Communist Russia

and the

Russian Orthodox Church

1943-1962

by

William B. Stroyen

THE CATHOLIC UNIVERSITY OF AMERICA PRESS, INC.
Washington, D. C. 20017

To Nina Ivanovna

Foreword

THE CHANGES in relationships between Church and State which were defined by the Soviet decree of January 23, 1918, ushered in a new era not only for the Orthodox Church but for all religions in the Soviet Union. More than that, the universality claimed by Marxist-Leninists implied the casting of the net of militant atheism out over all the world. In a certain sense, the rise of the "God is dead" theology represents a direct sequence of this effort. The revolutionaries in Russia did not annihilate God; they simply asserted that there was no need for the concept of God, that in fact modern man had superseded God, that man is God.

Doctor Stroyen reviews the history of the interplay between the forces holding this theory and those who have remained faithful to the God-concept. Since he is writing a scientific treatise and not preaching a sermon, he proceeds by analyzing the documents of the period rather than by theologizing. In so doing he reveals the factual problem faced by religious bodies in the Soviet Union, that their activity is restricted to worship and training for worship, whereas their opponents can, and do, avail themselves of every sort of measure which will create hostility toward religion and consolidate an atheistic culture.

This book provides information on the manner in which the Russian Orthodox Church has continued its life and service under these adverse circumstances. An important feature is the description of relationships developed by the Russian Church with Church life abroad. This is a case study of interest to anyone concerned with the interplay between Church and State in any or all countries.

Paul B. Anderson, Th.D., author of
People, Church and State in Modern Russia
(Macmillan), and Editor of the fortnightly *Religion in Communist Dominated Areas*, New York.

September 1966

Preface

The primary concern of this book is the interaction between the Russian Orthodox Church in Russia (the Patriarchate) and the Soviet regime during the period 1943–1962. A brief sketch of some events prior to these years is given for the purpose of historical perspective.

References to the pre-revolutionary period indicate that the position of the Church was one of privilege and prestige, however, not without State interference and control.

The first encounter of the Church with an atheistic ruler was ushered in by the Revolution of 1917, with the subsequent seizure of power by the Communists, who promulgated a program for the ultimate elimination of all religious influence in the U.S.S.R. In a series of covert and overt actions the internal administrative structure of the Church was changed, eventually reducing the Church in size and influence. The legislation of the State in 1918 and 1929, along with its intensive program of harassment, circumscribed the Church and severely limited it. The letter of these laws and the spirit of Communism still prevail.

The invasion of the U.S.S.R. in 1941 by the Nazis brought about a thaw in the Church and State relationship. After a series of conversations with the Kremlin leaders, directives were issued which incorporated rapprochement between the two institutions. None of the restrictive laws were abrogated; however, regulations were adopted in 1945 which guided the relations. Under this accommodation the Church increased its activities. Permission was granted to publish one monthly religious journal. The first copy was dated September, 1943. Eight theological seminaries and two academies were opened. The Church supported the war effort, and some clergy received decorations for meritorious service.

Since the end of World War II, the Church has again been put under mounting stresses and pressures. The main concern of this research has been the study of the interaction from 1943 to 1962 and has been centered on examining the monthly religious journal *Zhurnal Moskovskoi Patriarchii (Journal of the Moscow Patriarchate)*, other materials issued by the Patriarchate of Moscow, pertinent articles in the Soviet press and anti-religious literature.

The Patriarchate is amenable to the State. It participates in supporting the peace movement of the Kremlin. With the cooperation of the Kremlin, it maintains active relations with the Orthodox communities in other nations, and it is increasing its dialogues with non-Orthodox communities outside the U.S.S.R. This external sphere is expanding.

Internally, the sphere of the Church is narrowing. It has no freedom of expression, and it has no right of a juridical person. The Patriarchate is restricted to preparing ritualists for the Church; the number of operating seminaries is limited; the enrollment is also limited.

Communist philosophy has not changed; plans to eliminate religion in the U.S.S.R. are still operative as reflected in the anti-religious campaigns pursued in the press, schools, and literature. In 1961 the regulations of 1945 were modified, weakening the Church and restricting the Patriarchate.

Table of Contents

CHAPTER I

Historical Perspective

The Patriarchal Period. It was not until 1589, 136 years after the fall of Constantinople and nearly six hundred years after the introduction of Orthodox Christianity into Russia, that a Patriarchate was first instituted in Russia. This creation was partially due to historical circumstances which resulted from the fall of the Byzantine Empire. The Orthodox Church outside Russia was subjugated to the Ottoman Empire; it was weak and poverty-stricken, while the Church in Russia became influential and accumulated great material resources and status. When the Patriarchs of Antioch and Constantinople came to Russia in 1586 and 1588 asking the Czar's financial and moral assistance, they were queried on the possibility of establishing a Russian Patriarchate. By consent of the patriarchs on January 26, 1589, the Russian Church received its first patriarch who was Russian by birth and subsequently the Russian Church ascribed to itself the role of the "third Rome."

During the succeeding years, the Church[1] and the State became closely related. In 1613 Michael, the first Romanov Czar, sat on the throne of the State, while his father, Philaret, sat on the episcopal throne of the Church. This resulted in a diarchy which lasted until the death of Philaret in 1633.

Synodical Period. Some of the most extreme changes in the relationship of the Church to the State were ushered in by Peter the Great (1682–1725). His innovations caused great infuriation. For example, until the year 1700, the civil New Year was reckoned from September 1, which is the beginning of the Church year; however, Peter decreed that January 1 should begin the civil year. Adrian, the Patriarch, openly refused to officiate at the service appointed to signalize the decree's coming into force and Peter responded by isolating the Patriarch.

[1] When the word "Church" is used, it will mean the Russian Orthodox Church in Russia or the Soviet Union. The word "Patriarchate" will carry the same meaning.

1

The strongest opposition to Peter's reforms came from the established Church, for which he had profound contempt. His reforms, being Western in nature, did not coincide with the conservative traditions of the Church, which were Eastern in their origin. He introduced the reforms without consulting the Patriarch, thus defying the moral agent of the Empire. Patriarch Adrian responded to Peter's decisions by shutting himself up in the episcopal palace and allowing the administration of the Church to disintegrate. Adrian died in 1700 and with him the line of Patriarchs came to an end. Peter embodied the Church into a department of the State by establishing a Synod—a college or board of management—which was composed of bishops who were represented in the court of the Czar by an ober-procurator, a layman appointed by the Czar. He represented the Czar's policy and as the liaison he was able to interpose objections against the bishops sitting in the Synod and to advise the Czar if the decisions made by the bishops infringed upon the interests of the State. By the end of the nineteenth century the ober-procurator not only kept a check on the Synod but he completely dominated the administration of the Church, for he was the only official spokesman of the Church at Court. He kept the bishops under firm rule and imposed penalties on the clergy. The Synod remained the ruling body of the Church until 1917.

From the establishment of the Synod in 1721 to 1917, the Church bowed to the civil power by submitting to a series of written regulations which directed the members in their respective offices and defined the affairs which were to come within its jurisdiction. From the regulations it is very evident that the Synod was created by the Czar, its powers were defined by the Czar, and in the discharge of its functions it was made accountable to the Czar. As stated previously, it was composed of bishops and other dignitaries not elected by the Church but chosen by the Czar. Each member of the Synod had to take a special oath and declare: "I acknowledge the Monarch of all-Russia, our Gracious Lord, to be the final Judge of the College."[2]

Peter had informed the Patriarch of Constantinople of his decision to create the Synod replacing the office of Patriarch. In his correspondence he asked the Ecumenical Patriarch, as head Patriarch, to inform the other patriarchs and ask them to approve his (Peter's) decision. The Patriarch of Constantinople took two years to answer. However, when he did reply, he did not send the letter to Peter but to the Synod. He confirmed what Peter had done and gave the Synod the responsibility of the Patriarchal office.

Since the abolishment of the Patriarchate by Peter, each sovereign continued to exert himself over the Church. The changes which these

[2] Nicholas Zernov, *The Russians and Their Church* (New York: The Macmillan Co., 1945), p. 123.

sovereigns effected were in the realm of administrative discipline and not in the dogmatical. Of course, the administrative often affected the dogmatical such as the final control of the Church going into the hands of the Czars and away from the hierarchs by the creation of the Synod. The power of the ober-procurator increased, and bishops who did not conform were removed from the Synod. The Church and State became interlinked.

✱ This is clearly shown by Czar Nicholas (1825–1855), who published a decree in which he gave warning that he would take severe steps against any who attempted to injure the Church. He defined heretics and dissenters from the Orthodox Church as first cousins to the revolutionaries.

✱ The number of trials and severe penalties inflicted upon dissenters of all categories grew from year to year; according to official data, between 1847–52 there were five hundred verdicts a year against them, and the number of persons tried for belonging to the schism during these five years was twenty-six thousand four hundred and fifty-six.[3]

✱ The severe policy set by Nicholas I was to be followed until the end of the Empire. His successor, Alexander II (1855–1881), appointed K. P. Pobedonostseff (1880–1903) ober-procurator of the Synod. Pobedonostseff held firm convictions which became the guiding principles for nearly a quarter of a century in directing the destiny of the Church.

The traditional connection between Church and State is essential to their existence. Separation would imply the destruction of religion and morality, and the only Church which the Russian State ought to recognize is the Orthodox Church. Its adherents may be ignorant, its clergy rude and lazy, but it, and it only, is the Church of Christ, and it is as far above Catholicism on the one hand as it is above Protestantism on the other. Its duty is to keep itself free from entanglements with Churches abroad and to repress dissent and heresy at home.[4]

The authority of the ober-procurator in 1897 extended over 125,-688,190 inhabitants of the Russian Empire: 87,384,480 or 69.5 percent were Orthodox; 2,173,738 or 1.7 percent were Old Believers and sectarians; 11,420,927 or 9 percent were Catholics (Poles); 3,743,204 or 2.3 percent were Protestant (Baltic areas); 13,889,421 or 11 percent

---

[3] A. Kornilov, *Modern Russian History*, Vol. I (London, 1916), p. 297, quoted in Hugh Y. Reyburn, *The Story of the Russian Church*, p. 240.
[4] K. P. Pobedonostseff, *Reflections of a Russian Statesman* (London, 1898), p. 24, quoted in Reyburn, p. 257.

4   Communist Russia and the Russian Orthodox Church, 1943–1962

were Mohammedans; 5,189,401 or 4.1 percent were Jews; the remainder
were unspecified Christians and non-Christians. In the fifty provinces
of European Russia, however, the Orthodox formed a larger pro-
portion of the population or 81.8 percent of the total. In Siberia
the Orthodox formed 86.9 percent of the total population.[5]
⁕ In 1900 there were 49,082 churches in the Russian Empire. In addition to this, there were 18,946 Orthodox shrines and prayer houses.
To serve these places of worship there were 104,446 members of the
secular clergy: 2,230 cathedral deans, 43,784 priests, 14,945 deacons,
and 43,487 non-ordained psalmists. There also were monastic clergy:
16,668 monks and 41,615 nuns. The churchmen christened the 4,833,-
709 Orthodox children born that year; they married the 835,265
couples of this faith; and they buried the 3,069,766 Orthodox subjects
of the Czar who died in 1900.[6]

Dissatisfaction arose with the synodical form of administration.
The bishops openly manifested a desire for far-reaching reforms in
the administration of the Church.

On 23 March 1905, the members of the Synod sent a petition
to the Emperor for a convocation of Church Council and the restoration of the Patriarchate. Nicholas II expressed his approval
and, as a preliminary step, a Commission was set up to prepare
the Council's programme. A careful questionnaire was sent out
to all the bishops asking their opinion on the best ways of im-
proving Church life. . . . Only two diocesan bishops out of sixty-
two did not advocate its abolition (Synods). . . . The Conserva-
tives favoured restoration of the Patriarchate, the Liberals wanted
something more democratic.[7]

The desired change was postponed and the Church was even more
degraded during the time of the influence of Rasputin at Court.
Rasputin demoralized the members of the Synod, changed its membership and enraged even the members of the royal family by his
immorality. The Church under the Romanovs did not have an opportunity to recover from this last abuse.

⁕ Under the Provisional Government. When Nicholas II abdicated
his throne on March 2/15, 1917,[8] it marked not only the end of

[5] Tsentral'nyi Statisticheskii Komitet, Raspredelenie Naseleniia Imperii po
Glavnym Veroispovedaniiam, pp. 2–4, quoted in John S. Curtiss, Church and State
in Russia, p. 72.
[6] Sv. Synod, Vspeddaneishii Otchet, 1900, pp. 6–13 of tables, quoted in Curtiss,
Church and State in Russia, pp. 71–72.
[7] Nicholas Zernov, Eastern Christendom (New York: G. P. Putnams Sons,
1961), p. 205.
[8] The old calendar was used in Russia at this time, thirteen days' difference
from the current calendar. Thus this date, March 2, was March 15. A diagonal line
separates the two dates until the acceptance of the new calendar.

Imperial Russia but the loss of a legal protector for the Church. There was to be a change in the relationship between the Church and the State during the ensuing years, beginning with the Provisional Government which was formed on the day the Czar abdicated. ✶ The Provisional Government, which was in power for six months, was formed mainly of Octobrists and Cadets, with Prince Lvov as premier. It appears that everyone foresaw the revolution but no one prepared for it; destruction of the old forms of life was faster than the creation of new forms to replace them. Even in the Duma, the legally representative assembly, there were no clear ideas nor a political program. Endless and complicated negotiations continued until the Bolsheviks took over. It was a time when people were sick of the loss of lives in World War I; consequently, the question of war and peace was the primary concern of the leaders. Although on the whole the new leaders shared the feeling of the people, they recognized that occupation by Germany would be a deadly blow to the reforming spirit. The bourgeois parties favored continuance of resistance to Germany; however, the socialists pressed, with varying degrees of urgency, for peace. In May a new government was formed since the original leaders had made themselves unpopular with the masses because they favored continuing the war.

The Socialist Revolutionaries and Mensheviks replaced the bourgeois, and the Socialist Revolutionary lawyer Alexander Kerensky became Minister of War, replacing Milyukov and Guchkov, who had held the posts of Foreign Affairs and War, respectively, in the first government. Even the Bolshevik leaders were divided on this issue of whether or not to support the Provisional Government.

In April, 1917, Lenin arrived in Petrograd and immediately opposed the Provisional Government. At this time the Bolsheviks were not only unrepresented in the government but were also a minority in the Soviets. Yet by July Lenin attempted a take-over of the Provisional Government. He failed and was allowed to escape. Drastic purges of the General Staff ensued and by September Kornilov, the Supreme Military Commander, was treated as an enemy.

By the end of September the Bolsheviks had won a majority in the soviets of Petrograd and Moscow. In October they won over the troops in the capital. On October 25/November 7, 1917, the Bolsheviks ✶ seized power and a new government was formed with Lenin as Premier.

During this epoch the Church was forced to work out some plan which would permit it to function under the changed circumstances. ✶ In July, 1917, the Provisional Government provided for freedom of religious profession and the right to change religions or to profess none at all. This took away the exclusiveness of the Orthodox Church. The Church and government also differed sharply over the 37,000 parochial schools of the Church—one-third of the nation's total—which were put under the control of the Minister of Education on the grounds that they were largely supported by public funds.

✳ In August, 1917, in the six-month period between the overthrow of the Czarist government and the seizure of power by the Bolsheviks, the Church convoked a Church Council-Sobor to deal with the new problems forced upon it and the problems plaguing it from the Czarist era. The most important step taken was the re-establishment of the Patriarchate, which Peter the Great had abolished. The Sobor selected Archbishop Tikhon (Vasily Bellavin) to fill the post of Patriarch.

Archbishop Tikhon was an interesting choice since he had been a bishop in the missionary field in the United States for seven years. He was the son of a priest and was born in Toropetz, Pskov, in January, 1865. He entered Pskov Theological Seminary in 1878, and upon graduation in 1883 he entered Petrograd Theological Academy. It is noted that he was elected librarian by his classmates who had given him the nickname "Bishop."

Upon graduation in 1888 he was appointed instructor at Pskov Seminary. Almost the whole town attended the service when he accepted monasticism in 1891 and was given the name Tikhon. He was transferred to the Kholm Theological Seminary, where he served as inspector (dean) and subsequently became the rector and an archimandrite.

In 1898 at 34 he was consecrated Bishop of Lublin and Vicar of Kholm. Within one year he received his own see—Bishop of the Aleutians and Alaska in North America. It would appear that he was not very happy with this assignment because most of his biographies state that he accepted the see as his duty of obedience as a monk. His younger brother, who accompanied him to America, died there but was buried in Russia. Tikhon was in America for seven years, returning to Russia only once to participate in a summer session of the Holy Synod.

He became an archbishop in 1905 and two years later was transferred to Yaroslav, one of the oldest and most important dioceses in Russia. Later he was transferred to Vilna, where he resided until 1914 when war was declared. Since Vilna was in the war zone, Tikhon was forced to leave. He was able to take only the holy relics and some church vessels to Moscow for safekeeping. He settled in Disna, which was at the edge of his diocese, and spent much time visiting the sick and the suffering in the war zone. He received a decoration for this. Tikhon then became Metropolitan of Moscow and on August 16/29, 1917, when the Sobor opened he was elected Chairman.

It was not until the third ballot was cast for Patriarch that Tikhon's name appeared. When the name of three men elected were selected by lot according to the Apostolic tradition set for choosing Matthias, Tikhon's name was picked as Patriarch of Moscow and All-Russia. In spite of the fact that the Bolshevik Revolution had taken place, he was installed on November 21/December 4, 1917, in a magnificent ceremony in the Uspenski Cathedral in the Kremlin.

During the interval between the Communist uprising and the installation of the Patriarch, the Sobor, in keeping with its earlier attitude, showed open hostilities toward the revolutionaries. The utterances of the churchmen like the earlier actions of the Sobor suggested that the leaders of the Church had no intention of accepting the new regime. The Communists, on the other hand, were fundamentally hostile to religion and the Church. The future brought on a conflict between the two by way of anathemas and administrative decrees.

The churchmen did not seem fully to realize the intentions of the Communists; they were too immersed in their own internal struggle establishing a new administrative organ. Few of them were aware of the dynamic political struggles that were ensuing within the old empire; they had the problem of dealing with their own immediate needs. They were unrealistic in handling the social problems brought on by the abdication of Nicholas. They were also very complacent and never dreamed of the future without the Church and the czar's being the final victor. Tradition supported their dreams. These dreams are still held by many, even in the United States, who are convinced "Holy Russia" will still return.

The churchmen in 1917 did not fully comprehend that Communist vigor and vitality were powered by issues that contradicted God's existence. The curriculum in the theological educational system was centered on ritual and tradition, not upon psychology and the study of motivational attitudes. This resulted in a lack of adequate knowledge concerning current problems and the inability to see them clearly; consequently, in time, confusion was the order of the day. The Church leaders failed to foresee the possibility that it would hold a subordinate position to the future State.

Within a few years the churchmen realized that their ideals were frustrated; they were severely limited and had many new types of problems thrust upon them. The revolution spelled collectivism away from the Church's influence and the decay of the great traditional position the Church had once held by decree.

CHAPTER II

Beginning of the Communist Attack

✴ On December 4/17, 1917, the Communists began to pass laws restricting the Church. When all lands in the former Czarist Empire were nationalized by a decree, the law had specifically named Church and monastic institutions. This law was followed a week later by one which specified that all the Church schools, including theological seminaries with their possessions, were to be put under the control of the civil authorities. This went much further than the law passed by the Provisional Government, which on June 20/July 3, took over parochial schools which were supported by State funds. This December 11/24 law made no distinction between Church and State supported schools. Appended to this decree was a statement to the effect that the question of churches would be defined later in connection with the decree of separation of Church and State. The warning was noted by Church officials.

On December 18/31, a decree was issued which took away the vital statistics records from the domain of the Church. This decree also stated that only civil marriages would be recognized by the State and that Church marriages would receive no civil recognition. Divorce proceedings were taken from Church jurisdiction and placed under civil administration.

✴ These decrees infringed upon the domain of the Church, but they did not disturb the natural flow of Church life. The decrees affecting the Church continued. Early in January, 1918, the Communists confiscated the synodical printery; they closed chapels and made an effort to close the Alexander Nevsky Lavra (Monastery); and they removed all religious teachers from the schools.

On January 23/February 5, 1918,[1] the Communists issued a thir-teen-point decree which legalized the separation of Church and State. With this the Communists openly expressed their official atti-tude toward the Church. The decree circumscribed the Church and became the future guiding principle of the State in its relationship with the Church.[2] This decree still remains in the statute books though subsequent legislation has distorted it.

On the surface the apparent letter of the law shows no specific hos-tility, and it is difficult to understand how Marx's thesis that "religion is the opium of the people" and must be wiped out was to be effected; but it clearly shows the restrictions and limitations imposed upon the Church.

As a State Church the Orthodox Church had been receiving sub-sidies from the State. The cessation of these financial subsidies from the State was keenly felt by the central administration of the Church since its investments, its cash reserves, and its monastery lands had been confiscated, simultaneously eliminating the revenues the Church received from these institutions.

The Orthodox Church at this time presented a very formidable force. According to the 1914 report of the Holy Synod there were on the territory of the former Russian Empire 57,173 churches and 23,593 chapels—with 112,629 priests and deacons —500 monasteries and 475 convents with 95,259 inmates. The property and wealth of the Church was enormous. It owned 7,000,000 desyatins[3] of land and many commercial enterprises and houses. Its annual income was estimated to be about 500 million roubles. At the time of nationalization of the banks its deposits were about a billion roubles.[4]

This was not the first time the Church had suffered confiscation, but it certainly was the first time that the confiscation had been so thor-ough. According to the decree of 1918——

10. All ecclesiastical and religious associations are subject to the same general regulations pertaining to private associations and unions, and shall not enjoy any special privileges or subsidies either from the state or from local autonomous or self-governing institutions.

[1] The Soviet decree of January 26, 1918, adopted the Gregorian calendar and fixed February 1, 1918 (Old Style), to be February 14. After this change only one date (New Style) is used in this book.
[2] See full text of decree in Appendix A.
[3] A *desyatin* equals 2.7 acres.
[4] Julius F. Hecker, *Religion and Communism* (London: Chapman and Hall Ltd., 1933), p. 194.

11. The compulsory exaction of collections or dues for the benefit of the ecclesiastical and religious association is prohibited, as well as any kind of coercion or infliction of punishment by these associations upon their members.

12. No ecclesiastical and religious association has the right to own property.

They do not have the rights of a legal entity.

13. All property in Russia now owned by ecclesiastical and religious organizations is declared national property.

Buildings and objects intended especially for religious rites shall be handed over, by special decision of the local or central governmental authorities, free of charge for use to responsible religious associations.

✳ All holdings were confiscated except religious objects in the church such as chalices, books, antiminses, ikons, crosses, gospels, censers and other ecclesiastical properties needed for rituals and the celebration of the Divine Liturgy. Within a few years even some of these were to be taken for famine relief.

The decrees of the Soviet government created confusion in the administration of the Church. The newly elected Patriarch Tikhon issued a proclamation on January 19/February 1, 1918, while the Sobor was recessed for the Christmas holidays. This proclamation is structured into three distinct sections and is sometimes called the Anathematizing Proclamation. In the first part of his message Tikhon deals with the senseless cruelty and murders which were being perpetrated against the people in the country: "Reports reach us daily concerning the astounding and beastly murders of wholly innocent people, and even of the sick upon their sickbed." He anathematized those guilty and forbade them to present themselves for the sacraments.

In the second part of his message he wrote of the persecution against the Church. He stated that the sacraments of baptism and marriage had been pronounced unnecessary; that churches were needlessly plundered and destroyed; that monasteries were being made national property; and that seminaries were being used for purposes for which they were not intended. He implied that the Orthodox Church was singled out to bear the brunt of the persecution.

The last part of his message deals with instruction to his flock. He appealed to them to make their feelings known concerning their religion. He objectively stated that they might suffer for their action. He called the clergy to waste no time in asking the people to defend the rights of the Orthodox Church.

When the Sobor reopened after Epiphany on January 20/February 2, 1918, the Patriarch's statement received a general expression of approval. In fact, on January 22/February 4, the Sobor formally approved his message and passed an official resolution mobilizing with him.

Later, it condemned the decrees issued by the Soviet government and issued one of its own:

1. The decree issued by the Council of People's Commissars concerning the separation of the Church from the State is, under the guise of a law for freedom of conscience, a malicious attack upon all the structure of the life of the Orthodox Church and an act of open oppression against it.

2. All participation, both in publishing this legislation hostile to the Church, and likewise in attempts to put it into effect, is incompatible with adherence to the Orthodox Church and will draw upon the guilty persons penalties up to excommunication from the Church . . .

The Sobor calls upon all the Orthodox people now, as of old, to unite around the churches and monastic cloisters for defense of the outraged holy things. Both the pastors and the sheep of the flock of Christ will suffer abuse, but *God may not be abused.* May the righteous judgment of God come to pass upon the impudent abusers and oppressors of the Church, and let all loyal sons remember: we shall have to wage a fight against the dark deeds of the sons of destruction for all that is dear and holy to us Orthodox and Russians, for all without which life has no value for us.[5]

The Sobor and the Patriarch declared open war upon the Soviet Government and called on the faithful Orthodox to fight against it. The Sobor took on a militant tone and sponsored measures such as a great religious procession on February 24, 1918, to demonstrate the strength of the Church.

The Patriarch issued detailed instructions to the local churchmen concerning opposition to the decree of separation of the Church from the State which dealt with the nationalization of ecclesiastical property. In case of attack, they were instructed to ring the church bells and thus call the congregation to the defense of the Church. Consecrated objects were not to be given up voluntarily and, when seizure occurred, the persons guilty were to be excommunicated and priests who permitted the confiscation were to be unfrocked. As a result, parish brotherhoods were organized to protect ecclesiastical and monastic property.

Between February and May, 1918, hundreds of victims were killed in religious riots, and thousands were wounded and beaten; and, al-

[5] John S. Curtiss, *The Russian Church and the Soviet State* (Boston: Little, Brown and Co., 1953), p. 52.

though these demonstrations of religious strength were impressive, they failed in their ultimate objective. The Soviet Government continued to avoid a head-on collision with the Church; it concentrated on gradually establishing its administrative machinery. When it brought the country under its control, its position on the Church became firm and the clash soon occurred.

As the months went by, the hope of churchmen of a relaxing of the new Soviet law was dispersed by the restatement of principles at the Fifth Party Congress:

> The Constitution of the RSFSR adopted by the Fifth Congress of the Soviets on July 10, 1918, provided in section 12:
> "To secure for the toilers real freedom of conscience, the Church is separated from the State, and the school from the Church, and freedom of religion and anti-religious propaganda is recognized as the right of every citizen."
> Furthermore, along with the capitalists, merchants, former members of the police, criminals, and imbeciles, the clergy were deprived of the vote and the right to be elected—which relegated them to the category of second-class citizens and entailed serious limitations as to rations, housing, and other matters.[6]

On August 24 the People's Commissariat of Justice issued detailed instructions for the enforcement of the laws of January 23.

By late August, 1918, the Sobor dissolved because of the lack of funds and poor attendance; thus the burden of struggle was left to the Patriarch. He continued his opposition and complained about Soviet abuses. He issued a message in October, 1919, to Lenin and the Council of People's Commissars in which he summarized their rule. It is surprising that he was not executed. He sent the following message and arranged for its wide distribution.

> They that take the sword shall perish by the sword.
> This prophecy of Christ we address unto you, the present rulers of the destiny of our country, styling yourselves the People's Commissars. For a year you have held the power of the State in your hands, and are preparing to celebrate the anniversary of the revolution in October 1917 [sic]. But the torrents of blood of your brothers, mercilessly killed at your bidding, compel us to speak to you the bitter word of truth.
> Nobody feels safe, all live in constant fear of prerequisitions, robbery, arrest, execution. Hundreds of defenceless people are seized daily and lie for months rotting in foul prisons, are exe-

---

[6] James Bunyan and H. H. Fisher, *The Bolshevik Revolution, 1917–1918* (Stanford: Documents and Materials, 1934), pp. 511, 520–611.

cuted without investigations or trial, even with the simplified method of trial established by you. Not only are those executed who are found guilty towards you, but also those whom you know to be innocent, and who are merely taken as hostages. Innocent bishops, priests, monks, and nuns are shot on a wholesale, vague, and indefinite accusation of counter-revolution. This inhuman existence is made still harder for Orthodox believers by their being bereft of the last consolations of death, the taking of Holy Communion, and by the bodies of those slain being refused to their relatives for Christian burial.

You have promised liberty. Is that liberty when no one dares to obtain food for himself, to change one's dwelling, to move from town to town? Is that liberty when families, and sometimes all the inhabitants of a house, are evicted and their property thrown out into the street, and when citizens are artifically divided into categories of which some are destined to famine and plunder? Is that liberty when no one dares to state openly his opinion out of fear of being accused of counter-revolution? Where are freedom of speech and of press, where is the freedom of preaching? Have not many brave Church preachers already paid the price of their blood, the blood of martyrs? The voice of social and State discussion is suppressed. The press, with the exception of the narrow pro-Bolshevist section, is completely strangled.

It is not our business to judge of earthly powers. Any power tolerated by God would receive our blessing if it appeared as the judgment of God for the good of the people, and was not a terror to good works, but to evil.

But now unto you we tender one word of persuasion. Celebrate the anniversary of your coming into power by liberating the prisoners, by ceasing bloodshed, aggression, ruin, persecution of the faith. Turn from destruction towards the restoration of law and order, give the people the longed-for and merited rest from civil war. But now the blood of the righteous which you have shed shall be required of you, and you that have taken the sword shall perish by the sword.[7]

The Soviets responded to this critique by putting Patriarch Tikhon under house arrest and by marking him for vengeance. Confiscation of Church properties continued, and statements appeared in the press indicating how Church buildings were being used. The Communist operation continued.

[7] Hugh Y. Reyburn, *The Story of the Russian Church* (London: Andrew Melrose, Ltd., 1924), pp. 301–302.

CHAPTER III

Communist Operations

The Church in Russia learned from experience that the Communists not only had a theory about religion but that they took their theoretical philosophy seriously and put it into active and consistent practice.

Because the Communist ideology is monolithic, it leaves no room for any other philosophy of life—more than that, the Communist Party developed its ideology to the point that it became a "religion" which introduced a new way of life into Russia.

The open hostility of the Communists against religion has three roots. The first is the inherent materialism and declared atheism of Marxian social philosophy. The second is the hatred of religion which under the czarist regime was responsible for tyranny, the capitalistic exploitation of the people, and caused the most violent subsequent reaction. The third root is the new belief in the omnipotence of science as opposed to religion.[1]

It is out of this definitive ideology that the legislation against the Church in Soviet Russia continued to grow, for in Soviet Russia the Communist Party and the State are one. To rule in Soviet Russia one must be an avowed atheist in addition to being an outstanding and loyal member of the Communist elite.

The Communists regard that the sphere of activity of the clergy is, at best, limited to the residences of the members of the religious units and to the place where the religious buildings are located. They further state that only ritual can be permitted and tolerated and this only when it is sanctioned by the regime. This is illustrated by the laws and regulations (see Appendix).

Overt Action. At no point was Lenin more completely in accord with the values of Marx than in his attitude toward religion. He was

[1] Adolph Keller, *Christian Europe Today* (New York: Harper and Brothers, 1942), pp. 48–49.

a more violent and aggressive enemy of religion than even Marx and Engels. In 1913 he expressed the following attitude to Gorki:

> The difference between seeking God and constructing or creating or inventing, etc., a God is no greater than between a yellow or a blue devil. It is a hundred times worse than saying nothing to speak of a search for God, unless one intends to attack all devils and gods, all spiritual necrophilia; it makes no difference how pure and ideal or how created, not sought, he may be. The more refined and critical theology becomes, the more socially enticing and dangerous it becomes. (Such liberal theology is) the most dangerous vulgarity, the foulest infection, because every religious idea, any idea of any god, any flirtation with (the idea of) a god is an unspeakable vulgarity willingly tolerated and often enthusiastically accepted by the democratic bourgeoisie. A million sins, bestialities, rapes, and infections of a physical kind are more easily seen through by the crowd and therefore less dangerous than the refined spiritualized idea of God decked out in the most gorgeous costume.[2]

Lenin's formal treatment of the religious question is found in three essays: "Socialism and Religion," "On the Relation of the Worker's Party to Religion," and "Classes and Parties in their Relation to Religion and the Church." In his writings he protested against any compromise with religion. Lenin was not only a man of thought, but his mind was one of characteristically uninhibited vigor and his actions were coupled with systematic destruction of the religious institution. He believed the ends justified the means to the utmost degree. His goal was the complete destruction of the Church. In his modus operandi he encouraged every measure against the Church, the clergy, and the believing people in general. Reyburn observes:

> On 17th December 1917 revolutionary tribunals with unlimited powers were established to deal with all who opposed the revolution or were suspected of doing so. These are crowned by the All-Russian Extraordinary Commission for Combating Counter-Revolution. This tribunal gathers into itself all that was worst in the Star Chamber of England, the Inquisition of Spain, and the Council of Blood of the Netherlands. . . . The Bolshevist leaders made no attempt to check this butchery. On the contrary, they have encouraged it. In April 1918 Lenin complained: "Our rule is too mild, and frequently resembles jam rather than iron." Trotsky said: "You are perturbed by the mild terror we are us-

[2] Robert Pierce Casey, *Religion in Russia* (New York: Harper and Bros., 1946), pp. 77–78.

ing against our class enemies. Know that a month hence this terror will take a more dreadful form."[3]

The tortures and atrocities committed against the people are documented in Reyburn's book. He also notes that the Soviet regime was cynical enough to publish figures of execution in Russia since November, 1917, presumably covering a period of less than seven years. As far as the execution of church people was concerned, he observes:

> On the occasion of Tchitcherin's statement at Genoa that complete religious freedom reigns in Russia the Council of the Russian Church published a declaration recording the Bolshevist execution of 28 bishops and 1,215 priests.[4]

Cooke describes the reign of terror under Lenin as surpassing the French Revolution. In his book he quotes Norman Armour, the former secretary of the United States Embassy, who returned to the United States on November 5, 1918:

> Words are inadequate to describe what I saw in Russia during the reign of terror, misery, want, and wholesale murder. The people are starving and can get no hearing, much less redress, from the blood-crazed Bolsheviki.[5]

Special committees were organized by the Bolshevists to combat religion. Volumes could be filled with the accounts of the persecutions sustained by the religious leaders and believers. The following letter was sent to the Archbishop of Canterbury by the Archbishop of Omsk, the president of the Supreme Administration of the Orthodox Church, and was published in London on February 14, 1919:

> Having seized supreme power in Russia in 1917, the Maximalists proceeded to destroy not only the cultivated classes of society but have also swept away religion itself, the representatives of the Church, and religious monuments venerated by all.

> The Kremlin Cathedral of Moscow and those in the towns of Yaroslav and Simferopol have been sacked and many churches have been defiled. Historical sacristies as well as the famous libraries of the Patriarchs of Moscow and Petrograd have been pillaged. Vladimir, Metropolitan of Kiev, twenty bishops, and hundreds of priests have been assassinated. Before killing them the Bolsheviki cut off the limbs of their victims, some of whom were

---

[3] Reyburn, *op. cit.*, p. 289.
[4] *Ibid.*, p. 295.
[5] Richard J. Cooke, *Religion in Russia under the Soviets* (New York: The Abingdon Press, 1924), p. 127.

buried alive. Religious processions followed by great masses of people at Petrograd, Toula, Kharkov, and Eoligalitch were fired upon.

Wherever the Bolsheviki are in power the Christian Church is persecuted with even greater ferocity than in the first three centuries of the Christian era. Nuns are being violated, women made common property, and license and the lowest passions are rampant. One sees everywhere death, misery, and famine. The population is utterly cast down and subjected to most terrifying experiences. Some are purified by their sufferings, but others succumb.

Only in Siberia and the region of the Ural Mountains, where the Bolsheviki have been expelled, is the existence of the civil and religious population protected under the aegis of law and order.[6]

The Russian Civil War (1918–1922) brought on a prolonged period of intense suffering. The Church and the disenfranchised churchmen had a double yoke upon their necks because with the famine came the confiscation of the sacred vessels of the Church. At this time immediate and extensive confiscation took place.

The published reports state that the amount of gold taken was 442 kg.; silver, 336,227 kg., other precious metals 1,345 kg., 33,-456 diamonds weighing 13.13 carats; pearls, 4,414 gr.; other precious stones, 72,383 pieces weighing 28,140 gr.; 20,598 roubles in coins.[7]

The policy of confiscation expressed open disregard for the Church; the Patriarch denounced the action and called upon his most powerful weapon to combat it.

In the February 26, 1922, issue of *Izvestia* a decree was published by President Kalinin on behalf of the All-Russian Executive Council. This decree instructed the local soviets to remove from ecclesiastical property all valuable objects of gold, silver, and precious stones and to transfer them to the offices of the Peoples' Commissariat of Finance designating them for the Fund of the Central Commission for Aid to the Starving.

On the same day that the instructions appeared Patriarch Tikhon issued a reply. His reply was not made public; but on March 10, *Izvestia* stated that it had received a copy anonymously.

Patriarch Tikhon, in his encyclical letter, acknowledged the serious famine and stated that money had been collected in all churches

[6] *Ibid.*, pp. 128–129.
[7] Hecker, *op. cit.*, p. 209.

since the summer of 1921 to aid the famine-stricken people and that all sums collected had been turned over to governmental committees. He further stated that after a request was received for further aid in December even valuable ecclesiastical, unconsecrated objects had been donated. He then stated that he could not comply with the last decree asking for *all* valuable objects because, from the point of view of the Church, giving consecrated vessels was sacrilegious, and that he could not approve the removal of consecrated objects from the churches because he was prohibited by the canons of the Ecumenical Council which stated that consecrated objects could not be used for purposes other than the divine services and that the act of surrendering consecrated objects or using them for non-divine services was a sacrilege. A layman would be punished by excommunication, a clergyman by degradation from sacerdotal rank.

Patriarch Tikhon's encyclical was written on February 28, 1922, and he clearly cited from the Apostolic Canons, rule 73, and from the "Double" Council, rule 10.

The faithful responded to the Patriarch's Encyclical by resisting the order in Kalinin's decrees. Many offered to pay for the consecrated vessels. Many did not comply. Over 1400 incidents of conflict were recorded, many of which were noted in *Pravda* and *Izvestia*, especially those trials and executions which were held from late April through the summer of 1922. The manner of confiscation was no doubt provocative. The Church was surrounded by armed soldiers. The doors were closed, and only the pastor and the governmental authorities were permitted to be in the building. The officials did not show respect for the building or objects held sacred by the people, who often milled around the Church during the procedure. Many times, they did not remove their hats, used foul language or kept cigarettes dangling from their lips.

McCullagh describes the confiscation:

The Soviet Government calculated that it would get 800 million gold roubles out of the plunder of the churches, but it got much less, and most of the cash derived from the sale of what it got was not contributed towards the relief of the famine-stricken.

As a matter of fact, the Bolsheviks worried themselves very little about the famine. They never parted with a single one of the Crown jewels, which were valued . . . at a milliard of golden roubles. . . . They had not enough money to buy grain for the starving peasantry of the Volga, but they always had plenty for Communists in India, Persia, Great Britain, and the Ruhr. . . . And what did it get by its expropriation of altar plate? . . . A considerable quantity of altar plate was recently offered to a

Jewish firm doing business in Russia, but this firm, seeing that the speculation was a Commisar's private deal which had nothing to do with famine relief, and disliking to handle eucharistic vessels under such circumstances, promptly turned the offer down.[8]

Internal Church Conflict—Living Church. In continuing their antagonistic policy toward the Church the Communists enlisted the aid of a group of married clergy who were discontent with the results of the recent (1917–1918) Sobor. These priests, in turn, recruited a few bishops who were vindictive toward Tikhon. This group organized an administration with the goal of eventually removing or eliminating the Patriarchate. They became generally known as the Living Church.[9] However, they later splintered into innumerable fragments, almost every reformer founding a sect of his own. The Living Church leader, Bishop Antonin, was invited by the Soviets to join the Relief Commission as the official representative of the Church, and he readily accepted this appointment tendered by the government. By this appointment the Communists launched a new type of attack upon the Patriarchate which eventually paralyzed it. Thus, paradoxically, they became involved in "church business."

Bishop Antonin's appointment to the Relief Commission involved him in a trial in Moscow which was called the "Trial of the Fifty-Four." This trial began on April 26, 1922, and was completed on May 6. The indictment charged the accused with withholding valuables which could have been used to buy bread for the hungry during the famine in the Volga region. They were also accused of inciting riots and of committing counter-revolutionary acts against the government. The charges in the indictment were not validated.

The Patriarch appeared at the trial and said that he had no alternative but to resist the government decree because of canon law and to condemn the confiscation of consecrated objects by the government. He took upon himself full responsibility for the drawing up, publication, and distribution of his edict.[10] Nevertheless, eleven capital punishments were pronounced; of these five were carried out—all against priests.

Bishop Antonin appeared at this trial as a witness for the prosecution. As an expert in canon law, he stated that there was no justifiable reason by either ecclesiastical law or tradition for the Patriarch's edict.

During the "Trial of the Fifty-Four" the President of the court frequently spoke of the existence of the ecclesiastical hierarchy as

[8] Francis McCullagh, *The Bolshevik Persecution of Christianity* (London: Billings and Son, Ltd., 1924), p. 8.
[9] Also as the Church of the Regeneration, Union of Apostolic Churches, Revival Church, Union of Religious Communal Societies, and Free Labor Church.
[10] *Izvestia*, May 6, 1922.

being illegal. The official paper *Izvestia* read the same meaning into the decree separating Church and State,

> . . . The existence in this country of a "church hierarchy" as such is impossible. The decree allows the existence of separate religious communities, not joined together by any administrative authority and freely electing their clergy, who most certainly must not be confirmed by Episcopal Councils.[11]

This marked the beginning of a new phase in the State's relation with religion and the Orthodox Church.

Trials in other cities also had anti-Patriarchate witnesses for the prosecution. Priests Kalinovsky, Ledkovsky, Krasnitsky, and Vvedensky voiced anti-Patriarchal opinions at the trial of eighty persons in Petrograd in August, 1922. These witnesses paved the way for the subsequent breach with the Patriarch and, in a sense, a factual and open boycott of the Patriarchate. At the same time such trials inferred State encouragement and support for reformist groups of clergy. The first mention of the new movement appeared in the Bolshevik newspapers in conjunction with the "Trial of the Fifty-Four."

By the appointment of Bishop Antonin to the Relief Commission the Soviet State attempted to vitiate the Church and to give momentum to the process of its destruction by infiltrating from within. Bishop Antonin had a history of being involved in revolutionary actions. In 1906 he was relieved of his position as Bishop of Narva for this and, specifically, for refusing to pray for the Czar. He was sent for a rest to Voskresensky Monastery near Petrograd. Metropolitan Antony later gave him permission to live in the Alexander-Nevsky Monastery (Lavra) on a yearly pension of 1,500 roubles. He occupied himself with writing libelous pamphlets about bishops and members of the Synod. M. V. Lvov, Procurator of the Synod, had appointed him to Vladikavkas in the Caucasus in 1917; however, he never assumed this post because of ill health and had remained in retirement in Moscow. One of Patriarch Tikhon's first acts upon assuming office in 1917 was to send Antonin to Petrograd for a rest, but Antonin soon returned to Moscow. In 1920 Bishop Antonin became involved in organized public discussion with Lunacharsky, the Commissar for Education. He was also often called upon, by popular request, to perform ritualistic services. These public involvements brought him into contact with Kalinin, the President of the Soviet Union, and paved the way for his appointment as a member of the Relief Commission.

The arrest of Patriarch Tikhon in May, 1922, preceded the formation of the Living Church. It was easier for the members of this

[11] *Ibid.*

group to revolt openly against the Patriarchate when it was left orphaned and without a visible active leader and while Patriarch Tikhon was imprisoned in Donskoi Monastery, held incommunicado, and not informed of the current events of the Church. The Living Church decided to occupy, with the help of civil authorities, the vacancy thus created but they did not have the necessary canonical power. They made determined efforts to get authority from the incarcerated Patriarch Tikhon, who had since been quartered at the Troitzky Monastery. It must be pointed out that the Patriarch was not the only person arrested. Most of the Central and Moscow Diocesan Administration and Bishop Nikander, head of the Moscow diocese, shared his fate. Thus the hierarchal structure collapsed by ceasing to exist. On May 6, 1922, all the monks and servants who had lived with the Patriarch were arrested. His apartment and office were searched. Everyone who entered the reception room was detained and searched. Those who had documents on their person were sent to Lubyanka Prison; the others were detained for several hours and then released.

The leaders of the new movement soon promised their support to the High Political Administration or the G.P.U. in exchange for its protection, and they promised to act according to the command of the G.P.U.[12] Because of the cooperation and support of the Soviet powers they were able to capture the administration of the Patriarchate. The government placed at their disposal all of Zaikonospassky Monastery and permitted them to issue a religious newspaper—something the Patriarchate had never been allowed to do.

. . . The Renovated Church (Living Church) was decidedly favoured by the State. It held three Sobors, travel expenses of delegates to the first being covered by Government subsidy; it had acquired the cathedrals in principal cities with bishops in residence rather than in exile; it had maintained (up to 1927) two theological seminaries.[13]

Bishop Antonin had access to the public press. He published articles in *Izvestia* and *Pravda* stating that Patriarch Tikhon had transferred his authority to the Living Church. Since the Patriarchate was not granted the use of the same public vehicles for denying this statement, the Living Church for a time succeeded in being accepted as the Church body of Orthodoxy in Soviet Russia. Most of the bishops knew better and courageously rejected submission to this new administration, and many were sent to prison. Very few of the

[12] Cooke, *op. cit.*, p. 162.
[13] Paul B. Anderson, *People, Church and State in Modern Russia* (New York: The Macmillan Co., 1944), p. 75.

canonically consecrated bishops submitted to the Living Church because it openly sanctioned married bishops, second marriages for clergy, and marriage for former monks who were allowed to hold their original clergy status. These innovations were against the canons of the Orthodox Church and were most extreme. The Living Church proceeded to eliminate the potentially disloyal as it was trying to assure itself concord for its future existence and development under the Soviets.

In March, 1923, the Living Church convoked a Sobor. This Sobor made no revisions of doctrine or theology. Its main concern appeared to be twofold: to condemn Patriarch Tikhon and to express absolute loyalty to the Soviet regime. This they did. Patriarch Tikhon was "unfrocked," and loyalty to the Soviet regime was enacted by resolution. The Sobor closed on May 9, 1923.[14] The Communists succeeded in accomplishing a split in the Church, and in this manner they weakened the Church considerably both internally and externally. After the Sobor, the Soviet State made it clear that it did not condone the Living Church, and its policy toward religion continued.

Patriarch Tikhon's trial was to be held on April 23, 1923, while the Sobor of the Living Church group was still in session. After his imprisonment his health had failed him and there is no doubt that he was seriously disturbed over the events of the past year. He recanted his former anti-Soviet position in a statement:

> . . . I repent my offences against the Constitution of the State, and beg the Supreme Court to free me from custody.

> Henceforth I am no enemy of the Soviet Government. . . .[15]

To this was added another statement made by the Soviet Russian Telegraph Agency. The Agency's correspondent said that Patriarch Tikhon had made this statement to him.

> While kept in custody I suffered no restraint except, of course, the prohibition to conduct services. Communications in the foreign press alleging that I was tortured are absurd; my treatment was of the best. I have completely adopted the Soviet platform, and consider that the Church must be non-political. If the news that the prelates who have gone abroad are engaging in counter-revolutionary activity proves true, I propose that they cease such work as incompatible with the pastoral office. I think they will listen to me.[16]

[14] Cooke, *op. cit.*, p. 188.
[15] McCullagh, *op. cit.*, p. 72.
[16] *Ibid.*, p. 73.

After Patriarch Tikhon terminated his personal hostility against the Soviet regime and came to terms with it, all talk about his trial ceased.

The head of the Living Church, Bishop Antonin, was deposed by Patriarch Tikhon and dissensions soon broke out in the ranks of the Living Church. Patriarch Tikhon, after his release, condemned the Living Church and its adherents, and publicly announced, in a proclamation on July 23, 1923, that the Sobor which they held while he was in prison was null and void. At the time of this proclamation neither the Patriarchate nor the Living Church was favored by the Soviet State. On July 4, 1923, *Izvestia* carried an article which was summarized by Szczesniak.

> . . . In Church matters the State takes up a neutral position. "But the Communist Party is not neutral. All its views are diametrically opposed to the views and aims of the Church. The Party will always oppose the influence of the Church (no matter which Church), for that influence . . . bars the road to emancipation of mankind from the yoke of idols and tyrants, on earth and in heaven, real or imagined. The Church is dead. . . ."[17]

Anti-religious campaigns were continuous during this early period in Soviet Russia. *Pravda* and *Izvestia* carried the news of the campaign as well as incriminatory articles by Bishop Antonin about other reformers. Other items that appeared in these papers concerned the number of clergy who voluntarily discarded their robes and the closing of churches. The uprising of the peasants against the Church was also noted, and full coverage was given to the disputes in which the Church was involved. A vigorous and consistent campaign to destroy the sacred image of the Church was in effect.

The Living Church did not cease to exist after the proclamation against it by Patriarch Tikhon but continued to compete with the Patriarchate until World War II. However, the July 1, 1923, copy of *Izvestia* carried the Supreme Church Council's (Living Church) announcement that it had decided to dispense with the services of Antonin.

Patriarch Tikhon died April 7, 1925. His death was a severe blow to the Church. The Living Church took advantage of the situation and tried to strengthen its position by making many appeals for reunion.

Patriarch Tikhon willed that Metropolitan Peter be his successor. Peter's administration did not prove to be sufficiently subservient to the Soviets and he was jailed in December, 1925, when he delegated

---

[17] Boleslaw Szczesniak (ed. and trans.), *The Russian Revolution and Religion* (Notre Dame: University of Notre Dame Press, 1959), p. 191.

the authority vested in him by Patriarch Tikhon to Metropolitan Sergei of Nizhni Novgorod.[18]

Metropolitan Sergei held similar views to those of his predecessors concerning the Living Church; however, he stated that the group was not heretical but simply uncanonical. In effect he was saying that it had no binding powers because it was not legally constituted; nevertheless, his views did not change the relationship between the two churches; the conflict and competition continued.

Sergei pledged loyalty to the Soviet regime; yet, he was arrested in December, 1926, and kept in prison for half a year. During his imprisonment, his successors were also arrested and exiled. Quite often the non-Patriarchal clergy brought about the arrest of the Patriarchal clergy. The uneven struggle between the two groups continued until 1927 when Metropolitan Sergei was released from prison. On July 29, 1927, he signed a document which very clearly defined his loyalty to the government, and he also denied all ties with the political-ecclesiastical groups abroad who openly opposed the Soviet regime. He sought recognition by the government of the Patriarchal Church as the legally constituted successor to the Orthodox Church which existed under the Czars. He also requested permission to convoke a Sobor.[19]

After the signing of the document of loyalty, Metropolitan Sergei was permitted to move to Moscow in 1928, and he was granted permission to set up the much needed central administration of the Church and to organize a Provisional Synod. There were no reunion efforts between the Living Church and the Patriarchal group at this time. No doubt, Metropolitan Sergei reflected on the past when he came to terms with the Soviet regime, for the period preceding his pledge of loyalty was one of intense militant atheism against the Church and clergy.

A picture of this period is drawn by F. A. Mackenzie[20], who visited many places of detention and prisons and was an eyewitness to the struggle. The Communist authorities gave him unusual freedom to travel throughout the country, and he was in touch with the religious and political situation. Mackenzie charged that without reservation the Soviets were most harsh, very difficult and deliberate in their methods, that they surpassed anything known in written history as torturers, and that the exile system was a brutal weapon which did not lie idle in their hands—churchmen just began to disappear—and people

---

[18] William C. Emhardt, *Religion in Soviet Russia: Anarchy* (London: A. R. Mowbray and Co., 1929), p. 144.

[19] Matthew Spinka, *The Church in Soviet Russia* (New York: The Oxford Press, 1956), pp. 157–160.

[20] F. A. Mackenzie, *The Russian Crucifixion* (London: The Gainborough Press, 1930).

were living in a grotesque nightmare with no recourse against the
arbitrary men who ruled the day.

In actual practice, one who offended the Soviets by carrying on
religious work was usually charged with counter revolutionary
activity, a crime for which death could be inflicted. Ten years
imprisonment was not unusual. The common punishment for a
murderer was six years imprisonment. In effect, to be a Sunday
School teacher was to commit a more serious crime than murder!
This surely was a paradox of stiff-necked fanaticism.[21]

Anti-religious organizations. The anti-religious campaign was intensified by formal organizations for combating religion. In 1924, just
prior to the death of Patriarch Tikhon, a new anti-religious campaign
was launched through the Communist Youth Movement. Literature
against religion began to appear in spite of a severe paper shortage.
In February, 1925, the Militant Atheist League was formed.[22] The
anti-religious journal *The Godless* first appeared.

In 1926 a special conference was called by the Central Committee of
the Communist Party for the expressed purpose of considering ways
and means for promoting and furthering propaganda against religious
beliefs. A great number of public debates were held on religion, and
travelling puppet shows and anti-religious museums were organized.

The Union of Militant Godless grew rapidly. In 1926 it had only
2,421 cells with 87,033 members, but four years later it had 35,000
cells with 2,000,000 members. In 1932, the Union of Militant Godless
grew to 80,000 cells with 7,000,000 members besides 1,500,000 Godless children which were not included in the first figure.[23] Within less
than ten years, however, their activities decreased sharply primarily
because the new generation was not very much interested in the older
generation's fight with the Church.

In 1927 Stalin made the following statement regarding religion to
the First American Trade Union Delegation, which clearly sums up
the anti-religious campaign and the use of organizations to this end
during this period:

We conduct propaganda and shall conduct propaganda against
religious prejudices . . . The Party cannot be neutral with regard
to religion, and it conducts anti-religious propaganda against any
and all religious prejudices. . . . Have we oppressed the reac-

[21] *Ibid.*, p. 37.
[22] J. B. Barron and H. M. Waddams, *Communism and the Churches: A Documentation* (London: SCM Press, Ltd., 1950), p. 11.
[23] Serge Bolshakoff, *The Christian Church and the Soviet State* (London:
Society for Promoting of Christian Knowledge, 1924), pp. 43–45.

tionary clergy? Yes, we have oppressed them. The trouble is only that they are not yet fully liquidated.[24]

New regulations concerning religion are promulgated. There is no doubt that the Union of Militant Godless, because of its widespread activities and its great influence, brought to the attention of the government the need of new laws against religion. On April 8, 1929, a series of laws was promulgated by the All-Russian Central Executive Committee and the Council of People's Commissars for regulating religion. This detailed document, known as "Concerning Religious Associations", is still in force today.[25]

Although the Patriarchal Church under Metropolitan Sergei was officially registered in 1927 in the U.S.S.R., and thus received a right to legal existence, it was even more closely and easily watched in this obligation to the Soviets. The atheist groups were also more aware of it, which led to the regulations in the form of the laws of 1929. Under these decrees religious persons are permitted to organize if they are loyal citizens of the State, and they may be permitted to register their religious associations with the government, listing their membership, executive and accounting agencies. They may be given a building for worship if the government feels that there is one available, and they may be permitted to use it only if it is kept in good repair and if the government needs it for no other purpose. The building used for worship is continually subject to inspection by the local building inspector.

The decrees prohibit the congregation from creating mutual assistance funds or from levying any mandatory fees or collections from its members. The accounts of the congregation are subject to examination by government agencies, and the congregation does not enjoy the rights of a legal entity.

The objects used in the performance of religious rites are owned by the government and are only leased to the congregation. The persons signing the contract are fully responsible for their upkeep and for seeing that the property is used exclusively for religious needs. The items must be returned to the government when the religious association ceases to exist, either by the decision of its members or by the decision of the government.

No program not directly related to the basic function of worship can be sponsored by the religious association. The group cannot organize religious excursions, assemblies, libraries, reading rooms, sewing circles, children's playgrounds, etc. The local soviet supervises the activities of the congregation and all of the facilities which it uses.

[24] Anderson, *op. cit.*, pp. 78–79.
[25] For the full text, see Appendix C.

The congregation can appeal (but is not a legal entity) only to the Soviet regime; thus, the religious group must appeal to the anti-religious, which is permitted to remove elected members from the agencies of the congregation.

The handbook of the Communist Party and the Soviet Government has the following to say concerning religion and the Church:

> Containing the decisions of the All-Russian Central Admini-stration Committee and the Soviet of People's Commissar RSFSR, "Concerning Religious Associations" of 8 April 1929 becomes a most important document regulating at the present time the religious organizations on the territory of the USSR.[26]

Anti-religious education in the U.S.S.R. Since 1929 anti-religious education has become a part of the curriculum of the public schools. The chief aim is to prepare the youth in anti-religiousness, enabling them to combat religion successfully.

At a meeting of the Executive Bureau of the Union of Militant Godless held on June 15–18, 1933, a report was submitted which showed that anti-religious instruction was conducted at the local level by means of lectures, courses, seminars, and correspondence courses. It also showed that six schools of higher education and twenty-six universities were set aside for anti-religious instruction. Scholarships were offered to the most promising students of these schools.[27]

The Church had no means to combat this because all religious schools had been closed and all religious education had been prohib-ited in all schools; furthermore, it had no right to print any religious material to counteract the flood of anti-religious literature and dis-plays.

Even after the Decree of 1929 the churches continued to be closed. The clergy and their families were under duress. They were excluded from all cooperative societies, which in some areas meant slow starva-tion, deprivation of pensions and, in general, loss of all privileges of citizenship. In addition, Stalin started his great purge of Party members in 1933–1934, and no one appeared to be safe in Soviet Russia.

The Church continued to be subjected to restrictions; however, a change soon occurred which produced a *peredushka*.[28] This new mood apparently resulted because the youth was not very interested in at-tending the anti-religious lectures. Little enthusiasm was aroused for or against religion—a period of apathy prevailed.

[26] *Kommunisticheskaia partiia sovetskoe pravitel'stvo o religii i tzerkvi* (Moscow: Gospolitizdat, 1959), p. 116.
[27] Anderson, *op. cit.*, p. 118.
[28] Breathing spell.

On April 24, 1934, a resolution of the Central Committee of the Communist Party acknowledged that indoctrination with official dogma was considered a bore by all students of Soviet schools and diverted them from social activities. Consequently, teaching the theory of Marx and Lenin was discontinued in grammar schools and substantially restricted in high schools, but was left almost intact in institutions of higher education.[29]

Stalin apparently changed the openly harsh policy because the terror of the purges still lingered and the ranks of the clergy had been decimated. He no longer considered the Church to be an influential menace or a threat to his plans, and to continue the openly harsh treatment could have aroused sympathy for the Church not only in those who had been indifferent or who had experienced the touch of the extensive purge but in other countries of the world.

A new Constitution was proclaimed on December 5, 1936. Several changes were made which affected the Church. Priests received full citizenship; nevertheless, they remained in Communist eyes as members of a profession "exploiting the backwardness and ignorance of the toilers."[30] They were in reality still considered to be second-class citizens. Even those who left their priestly duties and renounced God were seldom trusted by the regime. The stigma generally remained. The decree of December 29, 1935, permitted the children of priests to enroll in all grades of school. By 1937 the action of the government was less violent; however, clergy continued to be arrested and churches to be closed. Timasheff states that the following event which occurred in the latter part of 1937 might well be considered a precedent.

The Committee of the Communist Party of the Province of Ivanovo (north of Moscow) expelled from the Party and removed from his position the editor of the paper in Vichuga (near Yaroslavl) for advocating the forcible closing of churches; the action was taken because Moscow warned the Ivanovo authorities that such an attitude was helpful to the enemy.[31]

The observance of religious festivals was permitted by Stalin by 1938; he prohibited blasphemous plays and films. He permitted the manufacture and sale of objects used in worship; however, Sunday continued to be a compulsory workday until 1940. Churches were closed indirectly by levying exorbitantly high taxes and rents against them.

[29] N. S. Timasheff, *Religion in Soviet Russia* (London: The Religious Book Club, 1943), p. 48.
[30] *Komsomol'skaiia Pravda*, August 10, 1937.
[31] Timasheff, *op. cit.*, pp. 121–122.

In the July 1, 1939, issue of *Pravda* a reference to the trial of an atheist was made. One person was sentenced to eighteen months in prison and others from six months to a year of compulsory labor without imprisonment for organizing a "hooligan raid" at Easter on a village church.

This new policy was not the result of an official change promulgated by the Party but one of circumstances. After the purges began, Stalin wanted to impart several new images, one of which was for the expressed purpose of influencing foreign relations. To attain this end, he eliminated the earlier more openly violent measures taken against religion and was thus able to influence the many visitors into believing that there was freedom of religion. Second, by the middle 1930's the Church was considerably weakened and to keep on violently beating what remained could incite hatred of the Soviet regime. No doubt, the acknowledgment of religion on the part of so many citizens in the census of January 6, 1937, also indicated that a modified policy was needed.

It must be remembered that this new policy was not an official change, but rather an implementation based upon expediency. Religious freedom was not actual nor intended by this new mood. Antireligious propaganda continued in a new or revised form, while religious propaganda was prohibited. Apparently, the leaders of the State decided that it was easier to manage religion when it was kept within the limits and controls set by the State through a centralized agency.

This policy also helped Stalin to control the atheistic elements of the Party, thus enabling him to rule with less potential power in the hands of any given group. Members of the Party and of the League of Young Communists were continually being reminded that if they participated in any religious rite they would be expelled from the Party. They were also discouraged from openly interfering with the rites. This was quite a reversal of the earlier policy which apparently permitted the anti-religionists to break every rule of morality as detailed in *Chornaia kniga: Shturm nebes*.[32]

The State was in no way converted. It did not rest its case; it only changed its tactics of dealing with religion for it felt that a modification of policy was needed for practical purposes. Confiscated church buildings were not returned to the Patriarchate or to any other religious group, and no indemnity was offered nor was any apology given for previous anti-religious action.

The thaw sets in. The tensions in Europe, the Nazi invasion of Poland, and the war in Europe continued to reinforce the need of

[32] A. A. Valentinov, *The Black Book: The Storming of Heaven* (London, privately printed, 1925).

continuing the new tactical policy toward religion. These new emphases in policy proved to be a wise move on the part of the Soviets, who were soon involved in a life and death struggle with the Nazis.

Because religion had always been such an important part of Russian culture, it fitted in with the new image which the Soviets were endeavoring to present to the world at war. The image centered on historical relationships and Russian nationality rather than Communist international appeal.

There is no doubt that the Church leaders had become discouraged and downhearted as all mortals do when they are confronted with no hopeful alternatives. The new easements in policy brought forth a new ray of hope and that spark in their souls was soon igniting new endeavors leading the Church into new areas. They accepted the new challenge thrust upon them by the avowed atheistic leaders of the U.S.S.R. Although it appeared that the Soviet authorities were holding the fate of the Church in the hollow of their hands and could apparently crush it at will, they were unable to do so because millions of people still trusted and believed in God.

Invasion of the U.S.S.R. When the Nazis invaded the U.S.S.R., the Soviet regime had to make even greater allowances for the people within their borders. The Patriarch and the other religious groups moved very rapidly. On the first Sunday after the invasion, Patriarch Sergei prayed for the victory of the troops and immediately sent a message calling on all the churches in the Soviet Union to join him in praying and supporting through patriotic effort the defense of the fatherland and asking everyone to work for the defeat of the enemies of *Russia*.[33] The message was not ignored. The Soviet regime, within three months, completely silenced the anti-religious voices and the flood of literature once devoted to this subject ceased.[34] It was in the same vein that the strict curfew was lifted and Easter midnight services were conducted in Moscow. The Patriarch and the Church supported the war efforts of the government with great zeal.

There appeared to be a determination on the part of both antagonists to remove some of the obstacles which would permit cooperative interaction between them. There was a great need of permitting the circumstances to control both of them if they were to reverse the difficulties which were first thrust upon them by the opening day of the Nazi invasion on June 22, 1941. Their quarrels which had resulted from two diametrically opposed philosophies had to be quieted. It appeared that the issues which for nearly twenty-five years had separated them into open warring camps, and which had resulted in blood-

---

[33] Italics supplied.
[34] Timasheff, *op. cit.*, p. 137.

shed, torture, and wanton destruction, needed to be put aside. A new path was charted. It is this new course which this book proposes to examine.

Prior to the uneasy accommodation of the Church by the Soviet government, the Church was withering away because of the slashing attacks of the government. The Church did not really live at all. It worked the best it could under the persecutions during which many of its leaders and faithful were constantly harassed, were put to death or exiled. The Church welcomed the opportunity to relax.

The emergency of war changed the previous order and the Communists went about smoothing some of the more obvious areas of severe friction. New views were adopted which avoided the open unmasking of the real past and the present; these strategic moves clouded the real issues of the motives of the Soviet government by stressing the salvation of the fatherland: thus the government's atheism was obscured and camouflaged. In the government's drive to uproot the ancient Church they came to the realization that to continue their previous modus operandi might result in severe criticism by their allies and by the people they governed. This they could not afford. To avoid judgments which might be flung at their ears and denunciations of their anti-religious policies, the Communists came to realize that the drifting events were warnings which they must heed, at least for the time being, if they were to assure themselves of the future development of their communistic society and ideology. Still the fist was gloved in velvet and the mission to destroy the Church went on by setting severe limitations upon it.

CHAPTER IV

Beginning of Communist
Expediency

On the surface it would appear that the Church has arranged a strange alliance with the Kremlin. The year 1941 is the significant place to begin the examination that led to the talks which were held at the Kremlin on September 4, 1943, when Stalin and Molotov were hosts to Metropolitans Sergei, Alexei and Nikolai.

On June 22, 1941, when the Nazis invaded the U.S.S.R., Metropolitan Sergei, head of the Russian Orthodox Church, issued a pastoral letter "To the Shepherds and Flock of Christ's Orthodox Church" in which he emphasized the historical contribution of the Church in previous wars and called upon the sacrificial offering "even of life in defense of the sacred boundaries of our homeland."[1] This opening statement appears in the foreword of the first book printed by the Soviet press which contains the views of the Church and has been circulated throughout the Western world. A public statement was issued on the freedom of religious confession in Russia. We find the following statement made by Bishop Andrei of Saratov concerning this freedom: "The Soviet authorities never limited the freedom of confessing of the faith,"[2] indicating that he concurs with the view of the Soviet government and the actions taken by it since 1917. From other statements made in this book, it is clear that when church officials speak of freedom to worship according to the dogmas, canons, and rubrics, and freedom to perform the sacraments, they do not include freedom to organize temporal organizations or to participate in society as an organized value system. Religious organizations may not form orchestras, choirs, or other artistic circles; plan concerts, excursions, or youth groups; or conduct work among teenagers or

[1] *Pravda o religii v Rossii* (The Truth about Religion in Russia) (Moscow: The Moscow Patriarchate, 1942), pp. 15–17.
[2] See full text of statement in Appendix G.

32

women. All of the above activities are unlawful for religious societies and clergy.[3] "Our Church is cleansed from useless concern and organs not connected with it and is not hindered in developing its holy activities. No one prevents it from fulfilling the outline of its dogma and the canon of its services and sacraments."[4]

The Divine Liturgy (Mass) in the Orthodox Church is always served following a set, strict order of rules. Very seldom is a petition or prayer changed, inserted, or excluded. However, a special petition was inserted into the Divine Liturgy, which was read in the Russian Orthodox Church during the Second World War, seeking God's intercession and mercy against the enemy and calling upon God not to be angry or to look upon the unworthiness of the people. This special petition particularly requested assistance for the military and also requested forgiveness of sins for all those that may die upon the battlefield.[5] The Church prepared a special *moleben*[6] for asking God's intercession on behalf of the nation because of war conditions.[7] Thousands of patriotic sermons were delivered by the clergy and leaders of the Church.

On October 23, 1941, Metropolitan Sergei, along with high ranking governmental officials, was evacuated from Moscow and ironically enough found himself in the town of Lenin and Kerensky's birth, Ulyanovsk on the Volga. From Ulyanovsk, he carried on a heavy correspondence even though physically he was not in the best of health and was over seventy-five years old.

The years 1941 and 1942 were memorable ones because the conditions under which the Church found itself were less limiting. Even though there were curfews, midnight services were permitted and the churches held overflow crowds even at the risk of death from air raids.

Metropolitan Sergei was encouraged by the government to make contacts with the other Ecumenical Patriarchs. All of them responded and sent telegrams wishing success to the armed forces and personal wishes of success to Metropolitan Sergei. Among those responding were Patriarch Benjamin of Constantinople, Patriarch Christopher of Alexandria, Patriarch Alexander III of Antioch, and Patriarch Timothy of Jerusalem.[8] This response was important to the Church leaders because it expressed the feeling that these Orthodox leaders and their flocks were on the side of the Allies and in particular with Soviet Russia and potentially cooperative with Sergei.

[3] See Appendix C.
[4] *Pravda o religii.* . . . , p. 71.
[5] *Ibid.*, pp. 87–88.
[6] Prayer service for a specific purpose.
[7] *Pravda o religii.* . . . , pp. 89–92.
[8] *Ibid.*, pp. 262–276.

Metropolitan Sergei lost no time in making contacts with the Russian Orthodox Church in America through its representative Metropolitan Benjamin. The reception given to these contacts was cool.

The portion that suffered the greatest part from the Germans was the southern part of the Soviet Union—the Ukraine. Metropolitan Sergei made every effort to advertise the damages and desecration of churches and rapine action against the populace. He utilized every opportunity and implement available to him to gain the loyalty of these Orthodox people. The book *Pravda o religii v Rossii* contains many articles and photos which depict the desecration and damages against the churches and the people.

In November, 1942, he made contacts with the Rumanian military forces asking them to desist from participating with the Nazis and, in December of the same year, he contacted the pastors of the Rumanian Church asking them to influence their leaders to withdraw support for Hitler. During the Paschal season of 1943, similar requests were made to the Christians in Yugoslavia and Czechoslovakia.[9]

At home, Metropolitan Sergei spearheaded drives for the collection of money for the war effort. By the late summer of 1944, over 150 million rubles were collected through the Church. This did not include the value of services and donations of kind. This information was given in a letter signed by Metropolitan Alexei, sent directly to Stalin and later published in *Izvestia*.[10]

Many of the hierarchs and priests showed themselves to be brave, loyal, patriotic, and defenders of the fatherland. Metropolitan Alexei of Leningrad, second in rank to Metropolitan Sergei, rendered distinguished service during the Nazi siege of Leningrad for which he was awarded the "Defense of Leningrad Medal."

Another area of concern which took a great deal of Metropolitan Sergei's time was the recruitment of clergy whose ranks had been extirpated by the action of the Soviet government during the past quarter century, 1917–1942, and had not been replenished. It is impossible to find a listing of the numerical strength of priests or deacons. A reference to bishops can be found, but it is difficult to state specifically how many bishops remained in the Soviet Union. However, there is evidence that by the end of 1939 there were only four.[11] To be significant, this information must be compared with the last

[9] *Patriarch Sergei i ego dukhovnoe nasledstvo* (Patriarch Sergei and His Spiritual Legacy) (Moscow: The Moscow Patriarchate, 1947), p. 90.
[10] *Izvestia*, October 24, 1944.
[11] Vassili Alexeev, *Russian Orthodox Bishops in the Soviet Union, 1941–53*, Mimeographed Series No. 61 (New York: Research Program on the U.S.S.R., 1954), p. 5. (The title is in English but the content is written in Russian.)

year for which statistics were available. The statistics of 1917 reveal a significant area of change. At that time there were 130 bishops.[12]

Metropolitan Sergei utilized many opportunities to show his loyalty to the Soviet Union. In 1942[13] on the 26th anniversary of the coming to power of the Communists, he emphasized that at every Church service prayers were to be offered for those in authority. He asked all Orthodox to pray that the government might find wisdom in governmental matters and in particular to bringing the war to a successful and speedy end.

Meeting with Stalin. These efforts bore fruit for Metropolitan Sergei beyond his fondest dreams when Premier Joseph V. Stalin hosted him along with Metropolitans Alexei and Nikolai in the Kremlin on September 4, 1943. This meeting brought many significant changes to the previous uneasily concluded truce by Metropolitan Sergei in 1927, when he expressed loyalty to the Soviet regime but was not granted his request to hold a Sobor. The 1943 meeting in the Kremlin was held shortly after Sergei returned to Moscow from Ulyanovsk, where he had resided during the past two years. At this meeting, Stalin said the government would not hinder the calling of a Sobor for the election of a Patriarch.[14]

Further accommodations followed: permission was granted to print an official journal, *Zhurnal Moskovskoi Patriarchii* (*The Journal of the Moscow Patriarchate*)[15]—the first issue of which was dated September, 1943; approval was given to open up seminaries; recognition was given to the Church headed by Metropolitan Sergei as the only valid and legal representative of the Orthodox people, resulting in the eventual liquidation of the Living Church and all other Orthodox church groupings which had developed since the Revolution of 1917; and there was an immediate expansion of Patriarchal activities.

The legal position of the Minister of Cults. A Department of Church Affairs attached to the Sovnarkom[16] was established in October, 1943, headed by G. G. Karpov, who held the rank of a full minister. This department was to act as a liaison between the Patriarchate and Stalin, bringing to mind the role of the ober-procurator, "the eye of the Czar." The main functions of this department were threefold: contacts between Church and State; preparation of laws and regulations relevant to Church affairs; and supervision of the execution of the laws.

Because the authoritative positions in the Soviet Union are held

---

[12] Anderson, *op. cit.*, p. 120.
[13] *Zhurnal Moskovskoi Patriarchii*, No. 3, 1943, pp. 3–4.
[14] *Ibid.*, No. 1, 1943, p. 5; *Izvestia*, No. 210, September 5, 1943.
[15] Future references to this publication will be noted as *Zhurnal*.
[16] Soviet Narodnikh Kommissarov (The Soviet of the People's Commissariat).

by the Communists, the Patriarchate is now directly responsible to the Soviet Minister of Cults. This relationship is simple, clearly and explicitly stated in the Forty-eight Paragraphs accepted in 1945. It regulates Church and State relationships.

The efficient and well co-ordinated work of the Soviet State organs would be impossible without a single guiding and organizing force. The guiding force is the Communist Party and its militant headquarters, the Central Committee.

The Communist Party not only plays a decisive role in the preparation and adoption of decisions by Soviet state organs, but systematically controls the fulfillment of these decisions.[17]

These organs are accountable to the Supreme Soviet of the U.S.S.R. Such an organ is the Council of Ministers of the U.S.S.R. V. Kuroedov, like G. G. Karpov before him, is a minister of this Council of Ministers, and in this capacity he has broad powers.

The Council of Ministers of the U.S.S.R. is the highest executive and administrative organ of state power of the Soviet state; it is the Government of the U.S.S.R.

The jurisdiction of the Council of Ministers of the U.S.S.R. embraces all major questions of state administration in all spheres of the economic, cultural and political life of the country.

The powers of the Council of Ministers of the U.S.S.R. are defined in general terms in articles 68 and 69 of the Constitution of the U.S.S.R.[18]

The Ministry is vested with specific powers; it has the right to issue—in accordance with the procedure laid down—*compulsory* decisions concerning the maintenance of order and security. . . .[19]

Consequently, the Patriarchate should be expected to consistently reflect a close and accommodating relationship with the Minister of Cults, a Communist, who represents the State.

Patriarch Sergei. The most important decision of the Sobor held on September 8, 1943, four days after the meeting with Stalin was the selection of Metropolitan Sergei (Ivan Nikolaievich Starogorod-

---

[17] A. Denisov and M. Kirichenko, *Soviet State Law*, ed. D. Ogden and M. Perelman; trans. S. Belsky and M. Suifulin (Moscow: Foreign Publishing House, 1960), pp. 205–206.
[18] *Ibid.*, pp. 250, 253.
[19] *Ibid.*, p. 268.

sky) as Patriarch of Moscow and All-Russia. Nineteen bishops[20] attended the historic meeting.

Patriarch Sergei[21] was born January 24, 1867, in Arzamas about 250 miles directly east of Moscow. He came from a long line of clergy: his great grandfather was a bishop and in 1768 was appointed vicar-bishop of Moscow; his grandfather and father were protopriests. Patriarch Sergei entered the seminary in 1880. He was graduated and entered St. Petersburg Academy in 1886, where he was enrolled in the Department of History. In January, 1890, he accepted monasticism. He was graduated from the Academy the same year, and in June he was assigned to the Japanese mission. Three years later he was appointed docent of Old Testament at St. Petersburg Academy. A year later he was appointed inspector[22] of the Moscow Academy and head of the Russian Conciliar Church in Athens and made an archimandrite, the highest rank in the monastic priesthood. He received a master's degree in 1895 and returned to Japan as assistant to the head of the mission of the Japanese Church. In 1899 he returned to St. Petersburg as the inspector. Two years later he became rector and was consecrated a bishop.

In 1905 he was appointed Bishop of Finland. The following year he became archbishop and was invited to the sessions of the Holy Synod as president of the Educational Committee.

He wrote many articles for theological magazines. His master's dissertation was published twice, in 1895 and 1898. The title was *Orthodox Teaching Concerning Salvation*. The Sobor of 1917–1918 elevated him to the rank of Metropolitan holding cathedral sees in the cities of Vladimir and Nizhni-Novgorod. In 1925 he entered into the administrative work of the Russian Orthodox Church. In 1934 he received the title of Most Blessed Metropolitan and was permitted to wear two panagias,[23] with a cross preceding his entrance at public worship services.

He was elected Patriarch on September 8, 1943, and enthroned on September 12, 1943.[24]

From September 8, 1943, to Sergei's death on May 15, 1944,[25] the *Zhurnal* remained under his editorship and the content during that

[20] The titles bishop, archbishop, and metropolitan are related to the rank of bishop and indicate seniority, generally in terms of tenure. In voting power they are equal, each having one vote on decisions concerning the church in general. A patriarch is also a bishop by consecration, for in the Orthodox Church there are only three ranks of clergy: deacon, priest, and bishop.

[21] *Patriarch Sergei i eho. . . .* , p. 14.

[22] Assistant to the rector.

[23] *Patriarch Sergei i eho. . . .* , p. 42.

[24] *Zhurnal*, No. 6, 1944, pp. 21–22.

[25] *Ibid.*, p. 3.

period showed that a rapprochement was worked out with the State. Letters and telegrams were sent to Stalin keeping him posted on the activities of the Patriarchate. The election and consecration of bishops, including their biographical sketches, the repentance remarks of the members of the Living Church, speeches and sermons by outstanding hierarchs, and learned articles of a politico-theological nature were printed in the *Zhurnal*. In addition, letters from the bishops, the clergy, and from the diocese were published; the main content related to the Church's support of the State's program and the people's sufferings under Nazi occupation.

The sixth issue of the *Zhurnal* of 1944 was dedicated to the memory of the late Patriarch Sergei. It contained many photographs of the funeral services and of the multitudes which attended. It also contained the sermons and eulogies which were delivered at the funeral service. The numerous telegrams of condolence received from the Orthodox Patriarchs were also printed.

On May 16, 1944, *Izvestia*[26] carried an announcement of Sergei's death and the plans for his burial and on May 20[27] reprinted the message of condolence from the Sovnarkom. This issue also contained notations concerning the funeral service and listed G. G. Karpov among the notables who attended. This expressed the interest the Soviet regime had in Sergei and illustrated that the authorities considered this incident important enough to convey to the public the idea that Sergei was, even up to his death, officially approved by the authorities.

On May 15 (the day of Sergei's death), in the presence of the members of the Synod,[28] the last will and testament of the Patriarch was read. The first portion stated that his successor *locum tenens* should be Metropolitan Alexei (Sergei Vladimirovich Simansky) of Leningrad.

At this special meeting of the Synod the following decisions were made: (1) Alexei was to enter upon the duties of *locum tenens,* and his name was to be mentioned as such in all services, (2) there should be an annual commemoration of Patriarch Sergei in all churches, (3) the Administration of the Moscow diocese was to be given to Metropolitan Nikolai of Krutitsk, (4) the funeral service for Sergei was to be held in the Patriarchal Cathedral of the Epiphany, and (5) all diocesan hierarchs were to be informed of these decisions.

Patriarch Alexei. Metropolitan Alexei,[29] the *locum tenens,* was

[26] *Izvestia*, May 16, 1944.
[27] *Ibid.*, May 20, 1944.
[28] *Patriarch Sergei i eho.* . . . , p. 50.
[29] *Zhurnal*, No. 6, 1944.

born in Moscow in 1877 and was graduated from the Moscow University Juridical Faculty in 1899. He was graduated from the Moscow Theological Academy in 1904. Upon graduation from the Academy, he became inspector of the Pskov Seminary, and in 1906 he was made rector of the Tula Seminary and elevated to the rank of archimandrite. In 1911 he was made rector of the Novogorod Seminary and abbot of St. Anthony's Monastery in Novogorod. Two years later, he became Bishop of Tikhvin and was appointed vicar of the Novogorod diocese. He became vicar of the Leningrad diocese and Bishop of Yamburg in 1921, and archbishop and head of the Novogorod diocese in 1926. In 1932 he was elevated to the rank of the Metropolitan of Novogorod. One year later, he was made Metropolitan of Leningrad. Since 1944 he has carried the title of Metropolitan of Leningrad and Novogorod. He became a permanent member of the Holy Synod in 1943. He remained in Leningrad during the whole period of the blockade and received the medal "In Defense of Leningrad." This biographical sketch was noted in the *Zhurnal* and in *Izvestia*.[30]

The same day this brief biographical sketch of Metropolitan Alexei was published, a letter was printed in *Izvestia* addressed to the President of the Sovnarkom, Marshal Stalin, in which Alexei acknowledged Stalin as a God-appointed leader, and informed him of the last will and testament of the late Patriarch Sergei which stated that he, Metropolitan Alexei, be his successor. He stated that these were responsible moments in his life and that he felt it was necessary for him to state his personal feelings to Stalin. He stated that he would be guided by the principles established by Sergei: to follow the Canons and decisions of the Church from one side and an unchangeable loyalty to the fatherland and to the government headed by Stalin on the other side, to function in total unanimity with the representative of the Sovnarkom, and, together with the created Synod, to guarantee freedom from errors and incorrect steps. He further beseeched Stalin to accept his loyalty in the spirit in which he wrote him, that is, with a deep feeling of love and gratefulness.

On May 19, 1944, in his first circular letter to the hierarchs, pastors and Orthodox laymen, Metropolitan Alexei wrote that he would continue in the path set by Sergei and stressed strict fulfillment of Church laws and loyalty to the fatherland.[31]

Metropolitan Alexei remained as *locum tenens* from May 15, 1944, to January 31, 1945. He evidenced exuberance in his pastoral activities during this period in developing a religiously-orientated image

[30] *Izvestia*, May 21, 1944.
[31] *Zhurnal*, No. 6, 1944.

of the Church and in preparing for the first Provincial Sobor to be held since 1917.[32]

What were the prevailing conditions during the period of Sergei's death to the election of Alexei as Patriarch? Why did he write the letters to Stalin and the Orthodox believers?

It is generally assumed that social systems are composed of at least five elements: position, roles, relationships, norms, and statutes, and that when we are able to relate these elements to a given person and his institution we should be able to predict whether we might anticipate conflict, accommodation, or conformity. The Soviet system is primarily *gesellschaften,* i.e., it is principally concerned about having the individual serve the means and ends of a given institution and is concerned with the production of goods or services that assist the institution in attaining its goals. This is accomplished not because of the individual's personal desires but if necessary in spite of them. This was expressed by Metropolitan Alexei's impersonal contractual plans in which he denied seeking his own personal satisfaction but stressed his ability to be controlled by the needs of the social system, the State and the Church. In his statements, he acknowledged the typical structure found in a *gesellschaften* operation which stresses cooperation among the members rather than competition and which presents a hierarchial organizational chart in which positions and chain of command are indicated vertically rather than horizontally, to indicate that responsibility is to the echelon above and authority is downward; that is, to each successive lower echelon. This is further illustrated by the fact that Alexei was provided with ready-made decisions stemming from the rigid control and discipline demanded through the establishment of the Sovnarkom, thus placing him in a state of dependency upon the State. As a result of this, it should have been expected that he would display a great deal of cooperation and coordination with the State and in turn would expect and receive conformity from those entrusted to his charge in the lower echelon.

Two preliminary meetings were held prior to the Provincial Sobor of 1945. A meeting of bishops was held first, followed by a bishops' meeting with Minister G. G. Karpov. At the first meeting Metropolitan Alexei stressed the valuable contribution of the late Patriarch Sergei; he spoke of the historical development of the Patriarchate, the need for strict discipline and fulfillment of laws, and the need of keeping in close touch with the Central Administration of the Patriarchate.

---

[32] A Provincial Sobor-Council does not need the permission of the other Patriarch to convene because it is specifically related to the province of the given Patriarch calling it.

Our main purpose, as I have stated, for which we come here to this meeting of the Sobor, consists of deliberations to prepare for the election of a Patriarch.[33]

At this pre-Sobor meeting of bishops, regulations concerning the Church in the Soviet Union were read; a report of the Patriarchal activities was read; a report concerning theological education was read; and a report was also submitted by the editors of the *Zhurnal*.

Metropolitan Alexei further stated that a second pre-Sobor meeting would be held with Karpov in November which would consist of detailing and accepting the program of the forthcoming Provincial Sobor. The agenda, the reports, and the speakers were to be discussed. Detailed procedures were established, not only in relationship to the agenda but also what was to be said; a full rehearsal was held, and the standard procedure for enthronization of the new Patriarch was agreed upon.[34]

To deepen the emotional tone, movies of the last Easter services of Sergei, his burial service, and of the thousands of people who passed his bier were shown. Another film of the destruction and desecration of the churches by the Nazis was shown.

After the bishops' meeting and prior to the Provincial Sobor, the representative of the Sovnarkom, Minister G. G. Karpov, was host to all the bishops on November 24, 1944.[35] One by one the bishops went to his office and were introduced to him by Father Kulchitsky, the ranking priest of the Patriarchal Cathedral, in the presence of Metropolitans Alexei and Nikolai. G. G. Karpov shook hands with each bishop but did not receive or ask for a blessing, which is the customary salutation. After this G. G. Karpov reviewed for the bishops the historical development of the Church from 1927 and the declaration of Metropolitan Sergei and emphasized the benefits received: (1) the opening of the theological institute and pastoral courses in Moscow; (2) the permission to publish a journal, calendars, and necessary church service books; (3) the receiving of religious articles necessary for the use at various services; (4) the excusing of the clergy who were actively engaged in parochial work from military duty regardless of age; and (5) the gaining of tax relief and improved living conditions for the servants of the cult.[36]

At the end of the report he asked if there were any questions. There were none. There were only a few requests. The conference ended

[33] *Zhurnal*, No. 12, 1944, p. 7.
[34] *Ibid.*, p. 13.
[35] *Ibid.*, p. 16.
[36] *Ibid.*, p. 17.

on a note of harmony.[37] The fact that there appeared to be a duality at this meeting, the State represented by Karpov and the Church represented by the two Metropolitans, and the necessity of the formal introductions indicate a definite bureaucratic-authoritarian relationship typical of a *gesellschaften* system.

The holding of this meeting and the report given by G. G. Karpov appear to indicate that Metropolitan Alexei did not want to leave any gaps open for personal criticism against himself and, secondly, to show that the State's desires and requests should be known and fulfilled. The fact that nearly one-half of the bishops were of recent consecration and that communication had been very limited within and outside the hierarchy may have made Alexei wonder whether they understood the Church-State relationship. Apparently this was not to be opened for discussion at the forthcoming Sobor. It set the framework within which they were to function in order to maintain the cordial State-Church relationship launched by Sergei with the permission of Stalin.

The Provincial Sobor of 1945. The Provincial Sobor for which so much prior preparation had been made was held in Moscow from January 31 to February 2, 1945.[38]

Metropolitan Alexei endeavored to make this Sobor a show case. He invited all the Orthodox patriarchs in the world, apparently to show the canonicity and the solidarity of the Moscow Patriarchate and its influence.

During this brief period he consecrated twenty-one bishops and filled seventeen vacant sees so that by the time of the Provincial Sobor there were forty-six to fifty bishops or approximately ten to twelve times more than in 1939.[39] The greater number of these bishops had theological training and were selected from previously married clergy, rather than from the rank of monk as had been customary. They accepted monasticism only two or three days before their consecration. Seventeen out of the twenty-one were former married priests, and thirteen of the twenty-one were seminary graduates.

Over the centuries many Provincial Sobors had been held not only by the Orthodox Church in Russia but by Orthodox Churches throughout the world. These Provincial Sobors differ from the Ecumenical Councils (Sobors) because they are limited to national rather than to internationally composed groups. The main concern of the Ecumenical Councils, of which seven are recognized as such in the Orthodox Church (325–787), was with doctrinal and discipli-

[37] *Ibid.*, p. 20.

[38] *Izvestia*, February 3, 1945.

[39] It is difficult to ascertain the exact number of bishops because some came out of retirement, while others came out of the previously occupied zones; however, the number of forty-six to fifty is generally agreed upon by students in this field.

nary decrees. The Provincial Sobors, on the other hand, are concerned primarily with disciplinary decrees and do not create doctrine. The Ecumenical Councils carry very great weight in the Church, they have supreme jurisdiction, they are considered to be without error, they are absolutely binding, and their decisions set the framework for all Provincial Sobors.

As related previously, this Provincial Sobor of 1945 was preceded by two separate meetings: the first meeting of only bishops, the second an official meeting of bishops with a governmental official. The Provincial Sobor was composed of bishops, clergy, governmental officials, laymen, and guests; this is the standard composition of all Provincial Sobors.

One of the primary purposes of a Provincial Sobor is to adjust to a changed world. At the calling of this Sobor the war was rapidly coming to an end, which, in turn, would usher in new problems and possible crises. Apparently, the State and the Church were aware of adjustments that had to be made to establish future relationships. The core of this future relationship rested upon the election of a leader to replace the late Patriarch Sergei and to establish a durable and sustaining cultural-religious relationship which would undergird the discipline which was essential to a *gesellschaften* system. Councils have always endeavored to remove stumbling blocks and to establish legalized existence. The First Ecumenical Council met after three centuries of intermittent persecution of Christians; it was called by Emperor Constantine whose main purpose was to redefine the relationship of Church and State. The czars emulated Constantine and publicly observed the rituals of the Church. The Provincial Sobor of 1945 differed from previous Ecumenical and Provincial Sobors because, among other things, it met in an avowed anti-religious atmosphere.

The last legally constituted Provincial Sobor called in Russia prior to this one of 1945 began in August, 1917, by permission of the Provisional government, with its final ruling issued on September 12, 1918. It was terminated when the Central Administration ran out of funds. At the Sobor of 1917 most of the members were elected by indirect voting. Two ecclesiastics and three laymen were permitted from each diocese. Delegates were also elected by the monasteries, the theological academies, the army and navy chaplains, and the universities. In addition, the bishops of the dioceses and the members of the Pre-Sobor Council were ex-officio members. In all there were 265 clergy and 299 laymen claiming to represent 115 million Orthodox.[40]

[40] Curtiss, *The Russian Church and the Soviet State*, p. 27.

In contrast, the Provincial Sobor of 1945 did not indicate the procedure used in selecting or electing its representatives, nor did it indicate the number of people for which it spoke. The Sobor included 133 clergy and 38 laymen from the Russian Orthodox Church, in addition to 12 members of the hierarchy, and 21 other clergy and lay guests.[41] The Sobor convened for only three days instead of spanning several months, and it ended with a grand concert on February 6, 1945,[42] instead of disbanding for lack of funds.

The Provincial Sobor of 1945 appeared to re-establish and reaffirm the theme of Moscow's being the "third Rome." This concept is a significant motivational factor and key to understanding current trends in the widening of the international Church sphere of the Patriarchate among Orthodox and Protestants and the anti-Rome articles printed in the official journal. The idea of Moscow's being the "third Rome" proceeded from a historical precedent which was first set forth by the monk Filofei of Pskov, who wrote to Czar Basil III in 1510, following the marriage of Ivan III with Sophia, the niece of the last emperor of Byzantium, "for two Romes fell, and the third stands, and a fourth there will not be . . ."[43] Thirty-three guests from all over the Orthodox world were invited. Among those who came were Patriarchs Christopher of Alexandria, Alexander III of Antioch, and Callistrat of Georgia; representatives of the Patriarchs of Constantinople and Jerusalem; representatives of the churches of Serbia and Rumania; and their complements of metropolitans, bishops, priests and other personages.[44]

The opening address was made by Metropolitan Alexei, president of the Sobor, who spoke of loyalty to the fatherland and its leaders.[45]

G. G. Karpov greeted the assembly on behalf of the State. He said that the decisions of the Sobor were very important to the blossoming of the Church. He spoke of the work and wisdom of the late Patriarch Sergei and of the contribution which the clergy made to the war effort. He stressed that the State does not interfere in any way in the internal problems of the Church. He considered conditions to be very normal and satisfactory and wished that they would be maintained. The full text of his speech was reprinted in *Izvestia.*[46]

Reports were given on the contribution of the Church during the war years, on theological education, and on the regulations governing the "Situation of the Administration of the Church."[47]

[41] *Zhurnal*, No. 2, 1945, p. 47.
[42] *Ibid.*, No. 3, 1945, pp. 27–32.
[43] N. F. Kapterev, *Kharakter Otnoshenii Rossii k Pravoslavnomu Vostoku v XVI i XVII Stoletiiakh (Character of the Relation of Russia to the Orthodox East in the XVI and XVII Centuries).* 2d ed. (Moscow: Sergiev Posad, 1914), p. 15.
[44] *Zhurnal*, No. 2, 1945, pp. 46–47.
[45] *Ibid.*, pp. 5–7.
[46] *Izvestia*, February 4, 1945.
[47] See Appendix E.

A letter was sent by the Sobor to the State which stressed its appreciation of the State, wishing success to the military and the great leader, Stalin, and pledging continued and unstinted loyalty.[48]

An appeal, in which war and suffering were the general theme, was addressed to all Christians of the World.[49]

A third letter which was addressed to all people of the world was signed by all the guests of the Patriarch. This letter "raised its voice" against those who use force, especially the Vatican, which it said tried to protect Hitler. It chided the Vatican and said that the Christian religion should strengthen that which is good.[50]

A circular letter was also released by the Sobor which was very emotional in content.[51] It spoke of the need of supporting the State against the fascists and requested devotion to this cause.

Metropolitan Alexei was selected by a direct polling of votes, which was pronounced as unanimous.[52] This was done in a very short period of time. It is interesting to compare this with Patriarch Tikhon's election in 1917. He was one of three candidates voted upon. The final selection was made by an aged and venerable monk by drawing one of the names which had been placed in a chalice. Thus, it was left to "the will of God."[53] (Incidentally, Tikhon had received the fewest votes of the candidates selected.)

According to *Izvestia*,[54] complete accord and unanimity prevailed on all matters voted upon at the Sobor.

The guests were occupied with visitations to the various churches in Moscow. A stipulated formula was followed in greeting them, after which they were presented with a valuable gift. The total cost of these gifts amounted to thousands of dollars. Before departing Moscow, they lauded the Patriarch through numerous speeches.

The enthronization of Patriarch Alexei was held on February 4, 1945. At this splendid and festive ceremony, Patriarch Alexei received congratulations from all the Orthodox hierarchs present as well as from Minister Karpov. These congratulations included an embrace and the traditional episcopal exchange of three kisses. The festivities included separate receptions given by Patriarch Alexei and Minister Karpov.

From all that could be seen, heard, and read during these historic days, it was obvious that there was a change in the earlier (pre-war) extreme behavior of the State toward the Church. Minister Karpov was present everywhere and displayed satisfaction and pleasure in the

[48] *Zhurnal*, No. 2, 1945, p. 11.
[49] *Ibid.*, p. 15.
[50] *Ibid.*, p. 17; *Izvestia*, February 10, 1945.
[51] *Zhurnal*, No. 2, 1945, pp. 15–17.
[52] *Ibid.*, pp. 49–51.
[53] Curtiss, *The Russian Church and the Soviet State*, p. 38.
[54] *Izvestia*, February 4, 1945.

interaction. On the other hand, the Church group expressed its gratefulness concerning the State's attitude. The guests left with glowing reports. This was certainly not the same situation which had prevailed at the 1917–1918 Sobor. The new social change indicated a takeover of new functions by the State and the Church which created a new system and brought on additional authority and responsibilities for both of them.

Forty-eight Governing Paragraphs. The important processes which were involved in bringing about a future social and administrative change was the adoption of regulations by the Sobor. They consisted of forty-eight specific and detailed paragraphs entitled "Situation of the Administration of the Church."[55] These regulations established the lines of communication and indicated the processes by which information, decisions, and directives were to pass through the two social systems and the ways in which knowledge, opinions, and attitudes were to be formed, modified, or discarded. From these Forty-eight Paragraphs the decision-making apparatus was formally set up and modi operandi and vivendi were established. Yet these same Paragraphs guided the Church and helped it to retain its identity and to maintain a stabilized, standard interaction pattern by setting up the necessary machinery for boundary maintenance. A definitive social-cultural linkage was established, resulting in a process whereby various elements in the two social systems became articulate and were enabled to function as a unit in order to attain specific ends or objectives. These changes in the elements made for not only a change in the relationship between the two systems but brought about an equilibrium and normative relations. These Forty-eight Paragraphs further established the rules and guiding standards which prescribed what was socially acceptable or non-acceptable to the State. These became the norms within the system and established the hierarchal structure: Patriarch, Holy Synod, Diocese and Parish. A definition was given of what was expected in a given status or position status role; this in turn involved the power control of authority and influence. The Forty-eight Paragraphs further defined hierarchal and social rank by rating what was higher or lower and what was relevant. They also defined what was sanctioned by the State and what was required from the Church, and they also indicated the channels which were to be used by the churchmen in obtaining certain facilities.

In this way the State set the behavior patterns of the Russian Church for the future; the pattern of interaction followed the lines of cooperation and accommodation. There appeared to be a mutual interdependency, coupled with a common threat, and also cultural and social restraints involved.

[55] For the text of the Forty-eight Paragraphs, see Appendix E.

This document which makes for accommodation is an acceptable working arrangement which apparently makes concessions to the Church. The Provincial Sobor adopted it unanimously, without any question or discussion. It left little or no room for deviation or innovation. It strongly influenced the behavior of the clergy and demanded total patternistic interaction. It is apparent that there is minimum room for conflict and competition which, of necessity, could destroy the equilibrium. It was based upon authority rather than upon democratic ideas. Because of the relationship of the Church to the State, it is difficult to see how the Church could protect itself from being threatened or exploited for the benefit of the State. The welfare of the Church depended upon conformity of Synod and Patriarch to these regulations. The change agent was the State and the target system was the Church.

The "Situation of the Administration of the Church" or the Forty-eight Paragraphs were not a part of the Soviet Constitution; they are not even law, but simply regulations set by the Sobor to govern the Church in conformity to the Laws of 1929.[56] They can be withdrawn or modified at any time.

From an examination of the Laws and of the "Situation of the Administration of the Church," quite a number of facts are apparent which indicate severe limitations and a general weakening of the volition of the Church. First of all, the Church is isolated as a social system in the Soviet Union because no provision is made for the use of the mass media, for the control of its faithful, for freedom in developing curricula, or for freedom of social mobility. Religious education is prohibited. The clergy's activities are restricted primarily to the Church edifice: the performing of devotional services and the sacraments.

The letter of Soviet laws and regulations is severe, but the spirit of the law is even more demanding. The government of the U.S.S.R. cultivates an air of neutrality with regard to religion in the knowledge that the real assault is assigned to the Communist Party. *The Great Soviet Encyclopedia,* after observing that the Church exists legally in the U.S.S.R., points out that the "Communist Party, however, considers religion an ideology having nothing in common with science and therefore it cannot remain neutral. . . . The Party considers it necessary to conduct profound systematic scientific-atheistic propaganda."[57] It must be remembered that the Party is the sovereign power.

---

[56] See full text in Appendix C.
[57] "Religiia i tzerkov," *Bol'shaiia sovetskaia entsiklopediia,* 51 vols., 2d ed., (Moscow: Gosudarstvennoe Nauchnoe Izdatel'stvo, 1949–1958), Vol. L, pp. 642–643.

Professor Gsovski traces the legal position of the Russian Orthodox Church and arrives at the conclusion that:

> The concessions to the Russian Orthodox Church in the Soviet Union were never put in the form of law, nor were the restrictive provisions of the old laws abrogated. Concessions today still remain a matter of policy and not of law. For its recognition as a union existing only for the performance of the cult the Russian Church pays the price of giving active support to all campaigns of the Soviet government including International relations. . . .[58]

The Church in Russia seems to have had its idea of freedom of religion clearly defined. Archbishop Benjamin Fedchenko stated in *Pravda o religii v Rossii* that freedom of religion is freedom to pray, freedom to perform sacraments and freedom to hold other public church services.[59]

The document "Situation of the Administration of the Church" is prefaced by a statement to the effect that it (regulations) was accepted at the Provincial Sobor of the Russian Orthodox Church on January 31, 1945, and also by the following paragraph:

> In the Russian Orthodox Church the higher authority in the area of the teaching of faith, church administration, and church jurisprudence—legal formulation, administrative, judgment . . . belongs to the Provincial Sobor, periodically called, composed of bishops, clerics and laymen.[60]

This concept of the Church stresses that the Church is guided not through the infallibility of one individual, but through a system which permits the participation of a triune structure: bishops, clergy and laymen, thus implying a conciliatory arrangement of authority which has binding powers on the faithful regardless of rank. As a result of this convocation the Forty-eight Paragraphs have become legally binding upon every Russian Orthodox. The Forty-eight Paragraphs indicate conditional participation, which gives the Church restricted access to the culture and makes the Church a subordinate institution in Soviet society. The degree of access depends upon the role assigned to and accepted by the Church. In this conditional participation, sixteen paragraphs are related to the office of the Patriarch (1–16), six paragraphs are devoted to the Holy Synod (17–22), while diocesan activities are defined in twelve paragraphs (23–34) and the remain-

[58] Vladimir Gsovski (ed.), *Church and State Behind the Iron Curtain* (New York: Frederick A. Praeger, 1955), pp. xxv–xxvi.
[59] *Pravdo o religii* . . . , p. 288.
[60] *Pravoslavnij tzerkovnij kalendar na 1946 god* (Moscow: The Moscow Patriarchate, 1946), p. 58.

ing fourteen paragraphs (35–48) are related to parochial matters. These Paragraphs are a systematic exposition which relate a methodical discussion of facts and principles involved in reaching conclusions, and contain the elements of a treatise which have been accurately and carefully compiled to insure the maintenance of an organized, predictable and systematic continuity of conduct. There are corresponding agencies established by the Minister of the Cults wherever there are sees[61] established by the Patriarchate.

It is surprising that the 1945 issues of the *Zhurnal* which detailed the activities of the Provincial Sobor made reference only to the Paragraphs without publishing the complete text, even though the *Zhurnal* did contain speeches, reports and letters in their entirety. It can only be assumed that this document was circulated primarily for the benefit of the clergy of the Patriarchate in the Soviet Union because it did not appear in any other publication except the 1946 calendar of rubrics, and then only after a lapse of some time.

It took a long time to develop this treatise. The process was very slow. Its formulation began with the declaration of Metropolitan Sergei on July 29, 1927, and continued slowly for a period of nearly eighteen years, or twenty-eight years from the time of the ascendency of the Communists to power in the U.S.S.R.

[61] Administrative agencies.

CHAPTER V

International Church Sphere
Widens

Throughout the period since the end of World War II, peace has been little less than a paraphrase of Clausewitz's celebrated dictum, namely, the continuation of war with other means. Peace has not been a state of international repose and contentment. Peace has been a phase of—or, so to speak, a variation on—the power struggle. This struggle has been waged with nonviolent means. The Soviet Union has sponsored a series of propaganda campaigns which have become known as peace offensives or appeals for the cessation of weapon testing which aim at neutralizing the technological superiority of its opponents. In this conflict no weapons are considered unorthodox by the Soviet regime.

The Kremlin's foreign policy results from the Communists' fundamental aim of effecting world revolution and establishing Communist power throughout the world. Now the Communists rely primarily on the psycho-political modes of conflict. They are endeavoring to induce a guilt complex in the opponents—guilt about such things as armament, colonialism, and use of foreign bases with the intent of immobilizing their opponents. On the other hand, they employ the Pavlovian conditioned reflex theory to paralyze by terror or to pacify into complacency. This is done by the ringing of alternate bells, peaceful intentions, and the threat of nuclear holocaust. The Soviets, since World War II, have successfully widened the global dimensions of the battlefield.

Within the Soviet Union the Kremlin attempts to gear all the established institutions to participate in its fundamental aim of establishing Soviet power throughout the world. Among the active institutions utilized in the achievement of the Kremlin's goal is the Russian Orthodox Church known as the Patriarchate of Moscow.

50

The Patriarchate is thus linked and related to the Communist global mission. It must participate in the Kremlin's policy, while not appearing to do so in the eyes of its followers and the general public. This participation of the Patriarchate in the Kremlin's global strategy has become an essential aspect of its international operation. This dimension of the Communist program—its use of the Patriarchate and its leaders as instruments—has been intensified.

It must be stressed that these activities first began during Stalin's regime and that Stalin, who had been an Orthodox theological student, was well aware of the religious stresses on peace throughout the world. His background and experience were, no doubt, a major contributing factor in conceiving of the need to have the religious organizations participate in the fight for peace.

The difference between the Khrushchev and Stalin concepts of peaceful coexistence was not as great as some people think. Since Stalin, there has been a constant and increased stress on the peace theme, an unceasing campaign to identify that universally wished for commodity, peace, with the party's brand name. Communist propaganda today rarely stresses old-fashioned treason. There is generally no incitement to overthrow a government by force, none of the old Marxist clichés about the inevitability of revolution, the need for intensifying the class struggle, nor for wiping out the evils of capitalism. The stress on the peace theme in Soviet political warfare and the current tendency of Communist propagandists to de-emphasize the cruder forms of revolutionary agitation in Western countries in no way reflect a genuine softening of the Soviet attitude toward the free societies. The peace theme is a more refined technique of indirect penetration than the earlier techniques employed under Lenin and Stalin.

Apparently Khrushchev realized that the Soviet Union would have to relinquish the hope of some day conquering the West by arms because such a program would inevitably lead to a nuclear war in which both East and West would be destroyed. But he did not abandon the goal of world power. He merely decided to attain it by other means. The means include diplomacy, propaganda, and other forms of psychological warfare, economic pressures, mass subversion and above all the support of every institution in the Soviet Union, including religion, to weaken the will of the people of the West to band together against Communism.

The Communist political warfare has become increasingly sophisticated, subtle, and imaginative. Many of the newest methods are semi-covert or "gray" propaganda. At the same time Khrushchev continued to give guns priority over butter. The purpose of this peace campaign was not just to publish news but to distort it. This is abundantly evident in the *Zhurnal* where the Communists control the flow of information.

On the home front, the Communists mobilize their civilian population by stressing that the West is the aggressive force which is trying to foment war. Thus, they continue to be able to stress guns over butter. As long as a surprise attack of the magnitude necessary to wipe out the United States, NATO, and other overseas bases is beyond the scope of Soviet capability the peace offensive will continue.

This psychosocial war has as its aim the control of men's actions through the capture of their minds and emotions. The Communists hope to get mankind to desire peace at all cost. They stress that war threatens their personal security, prosperity, and happiness, and they are endeavoring to convince the world that they offer protection and relief from insecurity, misery and unhappiness. They do this by eliminating all information which could conflict with the impression that they are peace lovers for peace's sake. At the same time they stress that the West is a warmonger and an agitator.

The *Zhurnal* has never ventured any criticism of the Communist Party or of the government, or of the government's policy and actions. In one field the Church has been an instrument of the government. The Patriarchate is an avid supporter of the Soviet Peace Policy, and the *Zhurnal* gives impressive support by devoting many pages to it. There is no doubt that the Orthodox communicants as well as their leaders have a real desire for peace; however, it is a question as to whether independent judgment on international affairs related to peace has been arrived at by the Patriarchate. It is probably more certain that their participation in the Soviet Peace Policy gauges their loyalty to the regime, which results in more toleration for the Church on the part of the government. In the area of the Soviet Peace Policy one can see a definite image of the Church because the articles contained in the *Zhurnal* mirror, reflect, and echo the Soviet Peace Policy in the greatest detail. The statements on the participation of the Church in this area of international interaction and on the home front are carried more often by the Soviet press, especially *Pravda* and *Izvestia,* than any other activity.

No one can doubt that the loss of twenty million dead during World War II has had a hard and lasting impact upon everyone in the Soviet Union. No people want war, especially when the imprints of the last war are still there. With the development of the nuclear armaments which imply a total war, highly impersonal, in which everyone is a potential victim, there is a demand for total action to avoid war. The purposes of the Soviet Peace Policy appear to be: to maintain the existing boundaries of the Communist block; to consolidate the material and other gains that have been made both at the battlefront and on the diplomatic front; and to increase further these gains within their consolidated boundaries.

✳*Peace Movement.* The Church's aim has been, from ancient times, the often repeated petition—praying for peace. The most important public worship service, the Divine Liturgy, beseeches the worshippers, "In peace let us pray to the Lord," and interspersed throughout the audible and silent portions are petitions which ask for peace; while just before the end of the service there is a request of "Let us depart in peace." To the Church, peace means a condition which is essential to the wholesome development of the Church in the world. Interestingly enough, the word for peace and the word for world in Russian are the same—"mir." One can hardly doubt that the Church believes its future to be significantly related to the Soviet Peace Plan—though in many ways in the long-range plan of the State it appears paradoxical because a victory of the regime will bring about additional limitations of religion under Marxist-Leninist totalitarianism.

✳The work of the Church in the area of peace is carried on by the External Relations Department, which up until July 4, 1960, was headed by Nikolai, Metropolitan of Krutitsk and Kolomna, who also headed the Publishing Department of the Patriarchate.[1] Metropolitan Nikolai was not just a leading personality of the Church but was the closest and probably the only near equal to the Patriarch himself. Of all the leading hierarchs of the Patriarchate, Metropolitan Nikolai had during his time become the best known and the most traveled. It is significant that the Patriarchate has published his speeches not only in the *Zhurnal*, but in separate volumes from which translations have been made into many foreign languages. These speeches were on the subject of peace, and no other speeches have received such extensive coverage in print.

The object of this chapter is to examine and relate information concerning the area in which the Church has been a reflector of the government of the Soviet Union.

✳Because of the limited recognition based upon expediency rather than law, the Church constantly has to be on the alert to the missions of the State and has to adapt itself to these missions. The Patriarchate's enormous support of the Soviet war efforts, from 1941 to 1946, proved to the Kremlin that the Patriarchate was a leader among many of the peoples within the Soviet territory, and it further proved that the Patriarchate was its ally in war. This led to furthering the closer relationship immediately after the war by appointing leaders of the Patriarchate, first, to membership in war atrocity commissions and later to peace organizations. The Patriarchate, no doubt, was pleased

---

[1] *The Russian Orthodox Church: Organization, Situation and Activity* (Moscow: The Moscow Patriarchate, n.d.), p. 134.

to be recognized as a significant social institution while at the same time the Kremlin was satisfied with the Patriarchate's eagerness to serve on these commissions—a mutual need existed.

Because the first war-time Patriarch, Sergei, died on May 15, 1944, he did not participate in the "fight for peace"; however, in his speeches, appeals, and pastoral missives during the war, the hope for peace was always included and prayed for with the hope for a victory of the homeland over its opponents. There is no reason to believe, after reading *Pravda o religii v Rossii*[2] and *Patriarch Sergei i ego dukhovnoe nasledstvo*[3] published in Russian by the Moscow Patriarchate, that he would not have participated in the fight for peace as have his successors.

Patriarch Alexei and peace. Once the position of the Church in the U.S.S.R. was explicitly stated or implied, its sphere could be widened to peoples outside the country. This appeared to have taken place on July 8 to 18, 1948, when the 500th anniversary of the autocephalous Russian Orthodox Church was celebrated. A special commemorative issue of the *Zhurnal* was printed and it contained the first reference to peace as understood today—"defense of peace." This issue also contained speeches and summaries of the celebration. It also states that G. G. Karpov was present and in his official capacity he greeted all the delegates from every important autocephalous Church in the world (ten countries), exarchs from eight countries, and the Armenian Catholicos George VI and that he stressed the freedom of the Church and discussed the part that the Patriarchate would serve in the developing and strengthening of closer, friendlier ties within the Orthodox Church of the world in its capacity as the world's leader.[4] In this same issue the telegram which Patriarch Alexei sent to Stalin is quoted as drawing attention to the occasion and expressing Alexei's appreciation of Stalin's labor for the benefit of the Soviet Union in the name of peace and for the benefit of all the peoples of the world.[5]

The attending religious dignitaries from foreign lands were treated exceedingly well during this historic celebration.[6] ZIV 110's, the more luxurious Soviet cars, were put at their disposal and other "niceties" were arranged for them. The clergy-participants responded by calling all the Christians of the world to join them in the spirit of peace.[7]

The Kremlin was anxious to convey the activities of this historic

[2] *The Truth About Religion in Russia*, 1942.
[3] *Patriarch Sergei and His Spiritual Legacy.*
[4] *Zhurnal*, Special Number, 1948, pp. 5–6, 11–12.
[5] *Ibid.*, p. 13.
[6] The 500th anniversary of the autocephaly of the Russian Church.
[7] *Zhurnal*, Special Number, 1948, pp. 31–32.

occasion throughout many lands; all of the proceedings of this meeting were printed in two volumes, *Dejaniia soveschania glav i predstavtelei avtokefal'nikh pravoslavnikh tzerkvei.*[8] These volumes contain nine hundred pages of absolute text. The tone of this conference was that of an ecumenical gathering, and a day by day account is rendered in the volumes.

The peace movement grew in intensity. In February, 1949, Patriarch Alexei called for the defense of peace in response to the International Committee of Cultural Workers, who had proposed a World Peace Congress. In an article in the *Zhurnal*[9] he states that the Church blesses and upholds the Committee's proposal for calling an All-World Congress in the defense of peace. He recalls the horrors of war and that in July, 1948, at the 500th anniversary celebration the Church had stressed the call for peace in mutual accord with that of the Soviet government. Alexei further states that he welcomes the opportunity to protest against war and looks upon the defense of peace as a sacred duty and as a higher expression of love to the Fatherland. He closes his speech by calling for the defense of peace and blesses all the co-workers of peace on earth with the hope that the whole world will be touched by the light of true Christian peace and brotherly love.[10]

Patriarch Alexei continued in his campaign for peace. On October 2, 1949, International Peace Day in the U.S.S.R., Russian Orthodox believers gathered in churches to pray for peace and to hear a new message from their Patriarch. The congregations were instructed to pray and work for the benefit of the Motherland; they were told to redouble their efforts in the universal cause of peace. Patriarch Alexei's address was highlighted by many references to scriptural texts. He began with Psalm 28:11, "The Lord shall bless His people with peace," and ended with the last verse of the same Psalm.[11]

His sphere of contact was ever widening. Five months later on March 3, 1950, Patriarch Alexei sent an open letter to the Patriarchs of Constantinople, Alexandria, Antioch, Jerusalem, Georgia, Serbia and Rumania; to Archbishops Makarios of Cyprus and Spiridon of Greece; to Metropolitan Paisi, president of the Bulgarian Synod; to Archbishop Paisi, head of the Albanian Church; and to Archbishop Timothy, head representative of the Orthodox Church in Poland.

[8] *The Acts and Conferences Held by the Heads and Representatives of the Autocephalous Orthodox Churches* (Moscow: The Moscow Patriarchate, 1949).
[9] *Zhurnal*, No. 2, 1949, p. 3.
[10] *Alexei, Patriarch Moskovski i vseia Rossii. Slova, rechi poslaniia, obrashcheniia, dokladi, statii: 1948–1954,* Vol. II (*Sermons, Speeches, Messages and Addresses*), (Moscow: The Moscow Patriarchate, 1954), pp. 132–133.
[11] *Ibid.,* pp. 134–135.

He opens his archpastoral letter with: "Blessed are the peacemakers for they shall be called the Sons of God."[12] He charges that his readers, who are apostolic successors, have as their prime duty the responsibility of pursuing and creating peace on earth. He states that if they do not do this they become hirelings, permitting the wolves to disperse their flocks.[13] He poses the question, "So what shall they select to do?" He states that the pastors of the Patriarchate have already decided to become defenders of peace.

He continues by saying that it is time that all Orthodox proclaim that international problems can no longer be settled by destroying millions of lives and that they must fight for the cause of peace. He makes these requests of all Orthodox brothers throughout the world and supports his statements, that defense of peace is their sacred duty, by quoting biblical verses. Patriarch Alexei again touched upon the pastoral conscience of the hierarchs and near the end of his letter categorically puts forth the defense of peace as obligatory for the Orthodox hierarchy of the world.

He concludes this archpastoral letter by stating that the non-Soviets are wrong in their assessment of the problems of the world and accuses them of inhuman planning, basing this upon William Fogt's article "Way to Salvation", which was printed in the United States in 1948.

In this letter Alexei gives no room for the Orthodox prelates to choose, since he states that to refuse his position would be tantamount to being hypocrites. He requests a reply to his archpastoral plea and asks God's blessing upon the true Christian works which appear upon earth as peace, and in mankind as fulfilling the will of God.[14]

Alexei did not send this letter out blindly. Several years before he sent it, he had visited many of these prelates in their own countries when in 1945 he visited the Holy Lands, Syria, Lebanon, and Egypt and every patriarch except Patriarch Athenagoras of Constantinople. Many of them in turn personally visited the U.S.S.R. in 1948 for the 500th anniversary celebration or had sent representatives. Consequently, he knew many of them personally and no doubt was familiar with their local situations and activities. In addition to these contacts, Metropolitan Nikolai visited London; Metropolitan Gregori visited Finland; Archbishop Fotii visited Austria and Czechoslovakia; and other delegates visited Germany and the Far East.[15]

---

[12] Matthew 5:9.
[13] John 10:12.
[14] *Alexei, op. cit.*, pp. 136–139.
[15] *Zhurnal*, No. 7, 1946, p. 10; No. 8, 1946, p. 27; No. 11, 1946, pp. 5 and 14; No. 12, 1946, p. 4.

After the letter was written, visitations were stepped up. Delegates from the Moscow Patriarchate have visited many countries, including the United States. Several visits were made to Paris to see Archbishop Evlogii.[16]

Not only were visitations made but bishops were assigned to countries where there are only nominal numbers of Patriarchal supporters, such as in the United States where Russian Orthodox Churches not affiliated with Moscow are well established. The publications sponsored by the Patriarchate bear testimony to the large-scale propaganda carried out by them.[17]

Since the Patriarch's historic call "in the defense of peace," the *Zhurnal* has carried many articles on the peace movement and the emphasis is so great that each issue contains many articles on this topic. For example, the July, 1954, issue contains fourteen articles on this subject, listed in a special category. Actually, many articles not categorized under the peace movement have some reference to this theme. The *Zhurnal* is not alone in this campaign. All periodicals published by the bishoprics of the Moscow Patriarchate overseas as well as the autocephalous churches in the satellite countries contain articles on the peace movement.[18]

The speeches and letters on peace by Patriarch Alexei continued. He appealed to his own flock with archpastoral letters on July 1, 1950,[19] and on August 29, 1951.[20] He then turned his attention further afield and addressed the Third All-Union Conference of the Friends of Peace in Moscow on November 19, 1951.[21] He addressed the same group the following year at its Fourth Conference.[22] His messages reached groups not only within the country but beyond. On November 25, 1950, he appealed to all Christians of the world in defense of peace.[23] He made this same appeal to the All-World Conference in Berlin on March 1, 1951.[24]

When the Korean War broke out, Patriarch Alexei sent a protest to the Security Council of the United Nations denouncing American aggression in Korea and the inhuman killing of the defenseless Koreans by American aircraft.[25]

---

[16] *Ibid.* No. 2, 1946, p. 7.
[17] *One Church,* printed since January, 1946.
[18] Leu Haroska, "Soviet Policy Toward Religion after 1942," *Religion in the USSR* Series I. No. 59 (July, 1960), pp. 26–27.
[19] *Zhurnal,* No. 6, 1950, p. 3.
[20] *Ibid.,* No. 9, 1951, p. 3.
[21] *Ibid.,* No. 12, 1951, pp. 4–7.
[22] *Ibid.,* No. 12, 1952, pp. 3–5.
[23] *Alexei, op. cit.,* p. 141.
[24] *Ibid.,* p. 143.
[25] *Zhurnal,* No. 5, 1950, p. 3.

In these international speeches Alexei made clear that the Patriarchate agreed with the government on the need of defense of peace and urged everyone to join the peace movement. He bestowed his blessings upon this movement. He stressed the need for disarmament and liquidation of atomic bombs and bacteriological implements.

Patriarch Alexei made many speeches about the Korean conflict. Notable among these were those made at Zagorsk on May 9–12, 1952, when he was host to representatives of all the religions in the U.S.S.R.[26]

A review of Patriarch Alexei's speeches and letters from this time shows that he continued on the theme of peace and the need for unification of Orthodox believers throughout the world. The peace theme was evident in the address he sent to the All-World Assembly at Helsinki, Finland, in 1955, and at the Fifth International Conference of the Defenders of Peace which met in Moscow in May of the same year.[27] At the Conference he outlined the Church's participation in the peace movement during the past seven years. He mentioned the work which Protestant churches were doing in this effort and called on all Christians of the world to join him. He clearly stated that all religions in the U.S.S.R. were cooperating with the State in this movement as they did during the days of World War II. He closed his address by saying that he hoped that good would overcome evil, and that this hope would give courage to face the future.[28]

When the head of the Greek Church, Archbishop Dorotheus of Athens, protested to Alexei concerning the inhumanity of the British on the isle of Cyprus, the Patriarch replied by implying that the British were absolutely wrong, stressing his deep concern for the Orthodox inhabitants and indicating that he prays for their success in obtaining freedom.[29] The Patriarch continued to reflect the sentiments of the Kremlin, calling for disarmament and the banning of the atomic and nuclear bombs at the Fourth All-World Conference.[30] He greeted Professor Joseph Hromadka when he received the Lenin Prize for his work in the Soviet sponsored peace conferences.[31]

In 1959 the *Zhurnal* published the speech Alexei made at the plenary sessions of the Soviet Committee in the Defense of Peace.[32] In its October issue the *Zhurnal* noted that on the tenth anniversary of the peace movement, at the All-World Conference, Alexei was

[26] *Alexei, op. cit.*, pp. 155–156.
[27] *Zhurnal*, No. 5, 1955, pp. 30–32.
[28] *Ibid.*
[29] *Ibid.*, No. 3, 1957, pp. 3–4.
[30] *Ibid.*, No. 9, 1958, pp. 3–4.
[31] *Ibid.*, No. 10, 1958, p. 6.
[32] *Ibid.*, No. 6, 1959, p. 3.

one of the recipients of the organization's tenth anniversary silver medal.

In 1960 the *Zhurnal* noted that Alexei addressed the Soviet Conference of Disarmament on February 16.[33]

The July, 1961, issue noted that Alexei sent greetings to the First World Congress of Christians in the Defense of Peace, which met in Prague in June, 1961. This message reiterated that he prays continuously for peace and wishes them success in their deliberations. The president of this organization was Joseph Hromadka of Czechoslovakia. The Patriarchate's relationship to the Kremlin is evidenced by the telegrams exchanged with Khrushchev and the Congress on June 14 and 15, 1961,[34] on the occasion of this meeting.

From this summary of Patriarch Alexei's participation in the movement for the defense of peace it becomes obvious that he considers the peace movement a very significant variable in his interaction with the Soviet government and the Orthodox world. It furthermore appears to show that this participation has directed him into many new experiences, and that these new experiences brought many contacts not only with Orthodox and non-Orthodox within the country but with Orthodox outside the U.S.S.R. and with Protestants of various denominations, leading members of the World Council of Churches, and non-Christians. These contacts were occasionally made through exchange visits. It is interesting to note that during this period, when religious dignitaries were visiting the U.S.S.R., antireligious propaganda was notably lacking in the news media of the U.S.S.R.

Metropolitan Nikolai and peace. Patriarch Alexei was ably assisted in the peace movement by Metropolitan Nikolai of Krutitsk and Kolomna. His participation in this movement is better known to the Western world than that of Patriarch Alexei since Nikolai was more active outside of the U.S.S.R. His first international participation was in Paris in 1949. The main theme of his address was a call for united effort in the defense of peace, stressing that the Russian people love peace. At these sessions he was elected a permanent member of the committee of the "World Peace Council."[35]

Metropolitan Nikolai then attended and spoke at the Stockholm Conference in 1950, appealing to all Christians to fulfill their duty of loving one another and seeking peace. He demanded that atomic weapons be banned. The Stockholm Appeal to ban atomic weapons was also signed by Patriarch Alexei.[36]

From Stockholm, Metropolitan Nikolai went to Luhačovic, Czech-

[33] *Ibid.*, No. 3, 1960, p. 33.
[34] *Ibid.*, No. 7, 1961, pp. 32–33.
[35] *Ibid.*, No. 5, 1949, p. 14.
[36] *Ibid.*, No. 6, 1950, p. 14.

oslovakia, where he attended a conference and spoke on the same theme.[37]

He next addressed the Second U.S.S.R. Conference for the Defense of Peace. Here he condemned all forms of violence by one state against another.[38]

The following month he spoke at the Warsaw Meeting of the Second World Congress of the Partisans of Peace about the "insane arms race." He also called for mutual tolerance and respect, notwithstanding differences of political and social systems, for a stable peace.[39]

The election of Metropolitan Nikolai to the committee of the World Peace Council gave him additional occasions to widen his circle of influence on behalf of the Patriarchate. He attended the First World Peace Conference in Berlin in February, 1951, and the Second Conference in Vienna in October. At these he spoke against the remilitarization of Western Germany and Japan and in favor of progressive armament reduction.[40]

At the conference held in Zagorsk in May, 1952, where Alexei was host to all religions within the U.S.S.R., Nikolai spoke of the need for the coordination of all religions in the U.S.S.R. for the defense of peace. The proceedings of this conference had international scope since they were printed by the Patriarchate not only in Russian but were translated into French, English, German and Arabic.[41]

Nikolai again went to Berlin in July, 1952, for the emergency meeting of the World Peace Conference. He was subsequently elected a member of the delegation to the People's Congress at the Fourth U.S.S.R. Conference. In this capacity he went to Vienna in December, 1952, where he accused non-participants of hypocrisy. The following June his travels took him to Budapest and the World Peace Council. Patriarchal bishops from Byelorussia, Moldavia, and Latvia later spoke with approval of these sessions. The Catholics and Lutherans of West Germany were appealed to by Metropolitan Nikolai in August when in a radio address he asked them to adopt a peaceful solution for the reunification of Germany. The World Peace Council was held in Vienna in 1953; here Nikolai stressed cooperation with the West concerning peace. The Korean truce was in effect at this time.

The year 1954 saw Metropolitan Nikolai traveling to Berlin, Stockholm, and other cities. In Berlin he attended the extraordinary sessions of the World Peace Council where he broadcasted an appeal

---

[37] *Ibid.*, No. 7, 1950, p. 13.
[38] *Ibid.*, No. 11, 1950, p. 5.
[39] *Ibid.*, No. 12, 1950, pp. 12–16.
[40] *Ibid.*, No. 3, 1951, p. 9.
[41] *The Russian Orthodox Church: Organization, Situation, Activity*, p. 223.

to the Christians of Germany, United States, England, France, and Italy to cooperate on the issue of banning the use of atomic weapons. In Stockholm he stressed the need of approaching peace through the spirit of justice and love and not through the superiority of force in armaments as a means of solving international problems.

Besides these two contacts, he addressed the Conference of the Christian Democratic Union of the German Democratic Republic by letter[42] on the need for nations to help one another rather than deceiving, robbing, and insulting the weaker nations. The World Peace Council of 1954 was held in Stockholm on June 19 to 23, where Nikolai continued the theme on peace.[43]

The Patriarchate continued its theme. On June 26, 1955, Metropolitan Nikolai spoke at the World Peace Conference which convened in Helsinki on June 22 to 29.[44]

During 1955 the *Zhurnal* contained seven international appeals made by Nikolai in the defense of peace. In 1956 he spoke about peace in Norway, Sweden, and the United States. He arrived in this country on June 2, 1956, and in the next few days spoke in New York City to the Federal Council of Churches, gave a press interview, spoke in Toledo, Ohio, and made numerous other speeches.[45]

In 1957 he made a broadcast in German to the Christians in Germany stressing the need for reunification and the prevention of war.[46] In June he delivered a speech at the sessions of the World Peace Council in Colombo, Ceylon, concerning the struggle for peace; he also sent a message to the International Union of Students at Colombo.[47] He closed his activities in 1957 by broadcasting messages to the Christians of Finland and the Christians of Europe.[48]

In the years to follow, Nikolai's speeches continued along the same theme—defense of peace and calling for disarmament.

It is to be noted that Nikolai always introduces himself somewhere in his speeches as a representative of the Church.

Most of the articles in the 1950–1960 issues of the *Zhurnal* are directly or indirectly traceable to the peace movement. All the peace movement articles that are of international significance appeared first in either *Pravda* or *Izvestia,* and this is duly noted in the *Zhurnal.*

Among the international conferences noted is the one held in Dresden on May 9 to 11, 1960.[49] Mention is made that Metropolitan

---

[42] *Zhurnal*, No. 10, 1954, p. 28.
[43] *Ibid.*, No. 8, 1954, p. 18.
[44] *Ibid.*, No. 6, 1955, p. 28.
[45] *Ibid.*, No. 8, 1956, pp. 22–43.
[46] *Ibid.*, No. 5, 1957, p. 23.
[47] *Ibid.*, No. 7, 1957, pp. 37, 47.
[48] *Ibid.*, No. 12, 1957, pp. 27, 29.
[49] *Ibid.*, No. 6, 1960, p. 54.

Nikolai was absent and that a message which he had sent was read by Bishop John of Berlin.[50] This message centered around an attack on the United States as an aggressor in the Congo, in Cuba, and in underdeveloped countries. It is reported that fifteen nations sent representatives to Dresden.

July was a busy month. Seminarians and young professors attended the Youth Movement Conference at Lausanne, Switzerland, as observers. Representatives of the Patriarchate attended the Third World Conference[51] at Prague, which was addressed by Efrem II, Catholicos Patriarch of Georgia, and by Metropolitan Pitirim of Leningrad. In 1960 Metropolitan Nikolai asked to be relieved of his position as head of External Affairs. His request was granted by the Patriarch through the Synod, and a note of appreciation for his ten years of outstanding leadership was extended by the Patriarchate by citing his ability and success in the peace movement throughout the world.[52] Metropolitan Nikolai was replaced by Archimandrite Nikodim, who was immediately elevated to the episcopate.

Bishop Nikodim's[53] rise is so phenomenal and the position given him is so significant in the international affairs of the Church that a brief sketch of his life seems to be necessary here. He was born in 1929. His early education consisted of graduation from the "middle school" and study at the Rjasas Pedagogical Institute. At eighteen he became a monk. In 1949, at the age of twenty, he became a priest. A year later he began taking a correspondence course through the Leningrad Seminary. He completed his work by writing a thesis on *The History of the Russian Spiritual Mission in Jerusalem* and received the degree of *Kandidat Bohoslovija* in 1955. During this same five-year period he served as a parish priest and by 1954 he became dean of a cathedral. Between 1956 and 1959 he became an Archimandrite (next monastic rank to a bishop) and head of the Patriarchate's Jerusalem Mission. In 1959 he returned to Moscow to take charge of the Patriarchate's chancery, and on July 4, 1960, he replaced Metropolitan Nikolai as head of the External Affairs Department.

From July 9 to 12, 1960, a Stockholm Peace Conference was held at which representatives from fifty nations were present. Resolutions condemning the United States' aggression in the Congo and Cuba were drawn up. The eighth issue of the *Zhurnal* devotes pages 31–37

[50] He is now the Patriarchate's representative in the United States and resides at 10 East 97th Street in New York City.
[51] *Zhurnal*, No. 10, 1960, p. 24.
[52] *Ibid.*, No. 4, 1960, p. 54.
[53] *Ibid.*, No. 8, 1960, pp. 17–18.

to a summary of this conference. All of these articles also appeared in *Pravda* on July 14, 15, 16 and 19, 1960.

The *Zhurnal*[54] also shows that the Patriarchate was represented at the Kremlin's New Year party by Alexei and Nikolai; evidently all was going well.

Greetings were constantly being reprinted in the first section of the *Zhurnal* showing the width of the Patriarchate's world-wide influence. Greetings came from all Orthodox dignitaries as well as from Coptic and Anglican leaders. The World Council of Churches also sent greetings. These greetings took up space in each issue—peace was the theme of most of them.

The *Zhurnal* noted that a new friendship house had been dedicated in Oxford, England, in honor of St. George. On alternate days, services are offered by Anglican and Orthodox. On the other hand, attacks on the Roman Catholic Church were common.[55] The November, 1960, issue devotes pages 40–47 to a running account of Rome's association with the Germans and Nazis and tabulates other aggressions against peace. Several cardinals are cited. Cardinal Spellman is mentioned as one of the foremost aggressors and is said to have blessed Francis G. Powers' U-2 flight at Adana, during the spring of 1960, to spy on the U.S.S.R.

The 1960 issues attest to the fact that there is no attenuation in the peace movement campaign. Bishop Nikodim, Metropolitan Nikolai's replacement, visited the Protestant headquarters and bishops of the Patriarchate in Paris during October 30 to November 5, and he also visited other churches in France. He visited Geneva, where he was the guest of the World Council of Churches, and he spent some time in Bossey, Switzerland, near Geneva, where the Ecumenical Institute is located; there he also spent some time with the representatives of Constantinople. His purpose was to advance peace and understanding according to the *Zhurnal*.

Articles on peace written by clergy of all ranks as well as by theological students and laymen have appeared in the *Zhurnal*. Apparently all levels in the Patriarchate have been reached and are responding, thus indicating the fervor, tone, and the intensity as well as the depth of the peace movement.

The December issue contained an outline of Patriarch Alexei's visits to the heads of the Orthodox Churches in Damascus, Alexandria, Cairo, Beirut, Jordan, and Jerusalem.[56] He held a lengthy conference

---

[54] *Ibid.*, No. 1, 1960, p. 13.
[55] This attitude has been consistently carried on since the mission of peace was inaugurated at the July 8, 1948, Conference.
[56] *Zhurnal*, No. 12, 1960, p. 6.

with Patriarch Athenagoras in Istanbul. This is interesting in view of the fact that in 1945 he avoided Athenagoras; an article in *Time* magazine brought attention to this particular visit in 1960. From Istanbul he went to Athens and then returned to Moscow.

The *Zhurnal* for 1961 continued to carry a section on "Defense of Peace." An article on the peace movement continues to appear in every issue. Forty-four articles were related to this topic, while only two articles were related to theological schools and only one to church and monastery buildings. Most of the articles were directly related to international relations, relations with other Orthodox Churches abroad, and with the ecumenical movement. Everywhere the tone was pitched toward the defense of peace and peaceful coexistence.

World Council of Churches. When the Patriarchate was accepted and admitted to full membership in the World Council of Churches in New Delhi, India, during its Third Assembly which was held from November 18 to December 6, 1961, it widened its sphere of contacts and potential influence. The World Council of Churches[57] is the largest Christian non-Roman Catholic organization on the international scene. It states in its press release of April 27, 1961: "The World Council of Churches is composed of over 170 member churches (denominations) in 50 countries throughout the world, involving some 170,000,000 people. Practically all major Protestant, Eastern Orthodox and Anglican Churches in the United States are included."

The Patriarchate's application for membership grew out of consultations dating back to the days before the Council was actually constituted in 1948. From 1946 to 1948, the Council made repeated efforts to secure the participation of the Patriarchate. In 1948 the Patriarch informed the Council that it had decided not to join. For the next six years there was little contact between the Patriarchate and the Council. It was not until after the Second Assembly in Evanston, Illinois, that conversations were resumed, when the Council informed the Patriarchate of its interest in world peace and disarmament. Since August, 1958, the Patriarchate has sent representatives to various Council meetings. The Council headquarters have been in Geneva, Switzerland, since its First Assembly held in 1948 in Amsterdam. Their property holdings run into millions of dollars.

The *Zhurnal*[58] states that the Patriarchate was most pleased to become a member of the Council and that it is willing to have members in all departments of the Council which are devoted to seeking Christian unity and further states that the Council must endeavor to bring about peace in the world. This same issue carried an article

---

[57] Whenever the word "Council" is used in this chapter, it will represent the World Council of Churches.
[58] *Zhurnal*, No. 1, 1962, pp. 49–51.

by the Council entitled "Call to all Governments and Peoples,"[59] which tells of the Council's call for world peace. A section was devoted to "Ecumenical Problems."

On June 1, 1962, a Council delegation visited the Patriarchate in Moscow, its religious communities in Moscow, the seminary-academy at Zagorsk, and the churches in Leningrad, Tallin, and Tbilski. The July issue of the *Zhurnal* stated that the purpose of the visit was to become familiar with the details of church life in the Soviet Union. The Council was represented by six members who said that they were deeply impressed by the spiritual power of the people and their loyalty to the Church.

In August, 1962, four representatives of the Patriarchate attended the Council's sessions of the Central Committee in Paris. This trip was noted in the January, 1963, issue of the *Zhurnal*, which also stated that in addition to the Patriarchate, the Georgian Orthodox, two Armenian Apostolic, the Estonian Lutheran, the Evangelical Lutheran, and the Union of Evangelical Christian Baptist Churches and others in the U.S.S.R. belong to the Council.[60] These others, not named, are Orthodox Churches in the satellite countries.

Thus again the Patriarchate has set the path for other denominations in the U.S.S.R. There is no doubt that it will be active in the Council; however, it is still too early to determine how much influence it will have. It is the largest single member.

Relations with other churches. Broader and deepening cordial relations were evidenced between the Orthodox Churches when the leaders met at Rhodes in September, 1961. This was a historic event and the representatives from the Patriarchate were there as well as Orthodox representatives from all over the world. The Patriarch, along with a large delegation, visited the Orthodox officials in Yugoslavia, Bulgaria, and Rumania. These visits were made between May 21 and June 4, 1962. Representatives of the Patriarchate also visited Mt. Athos, the most ancient shrine of Orthodoxy in the world. From the articles in the *Zhurnal* in June and July, 1962, it becomes obvious that the Patriarchate's assumed role is one of leadership.

The non-Orthodox world was not forgotten. Archbishop Nikodim, head of the External Affairs Department, visited with Protestants and Roman Catholics in France and Belgium. He also held a conference with the head of the Old Catholic group, Archbishop Andrew Rinkel, at Utrecht, Holland, in December of 1961. Representatives of the Patriarchate also participated in the Conference of European Churches at

[59] *Ibid.*, pp. 58–59.
[60] This shows the number of the churches in the U.S.S.R. responding to the Kremlin's theme of peace.

Niborg, Denmark[61] (which, incidentally, is not a member of the World Council of Churches). At home, they were present at the Armenian Church Conference, which was held at Etchmiazdin in September.

Not only did members of the Patriarchate travel to conferences in various countries but these calls were often returned. The pastors and theologians from East Germany visited in April during Holy Week.[62] In May, Greek Orthodox Bishop Timadis visited along with theologians, among them Professor Alivizantos, who is renowned and active with the World Council of Churches. Michael Ramsey, Archbishop of Canterbury, was the Patriarchate's guest from July 30 to August 3, 1962.[63] He was followed by a delegation from the National Council of Churches of the United States, which spent several weeks in Russia as guests of the Patriarchate.[64] The Patriarchate then returned this visit by spending a few weeks visiting churches in the United States as guests of the National Council of Churches of the United States.

After the vilification of the Vatican in both the *Zhurnal* and the Soviet press, the new era of communication of the Vatican with both State and Church officials in Moscow appears paradoxical. Observers from the Patriarchate were invited by the Roman Catholic Pope to attend the Second Vatican Council in the fall of 1962. The Patriarchate was the only Orthodox group which sent observers,[65] even though this was contrary to the decision made at the Orthodox meeting in Rhodes in September of the previous year.[66] During and since the fall of 1962 the State has also acknowledged the Vatican, and Khrushchev's son-in-law had an audience with Pope John. Both Church and State appear to have made this new move concurrently.

The *Syracuse Herald Journal* carried an article by Tom Ochiltree on page 8 of its June 28, 1963, issue "Pope Paul Strives to Renew Red Ties." In it Mr. Ochiltree writes:

> In his week-old reign, the pontiff has set the stage publicly for re-establishing Vatican ties with Communist nations . . . Pope Paul reportedly is more interested in repairing bonds disrupted after World War II than in keeping alive old conflicts with Communists. In this he is following the policies initiated by Pope John XXIII.

Thus a new dimension is in the making which will also involve the Patriarchate in its fight for peace. Apparently, the immediate political

[61] *Zhurnal*, No. 2, 1961, p. 68.
[62] *Ibid.*, No. 6, 1962, p. 23.
[63] *Ibid.*, No. 9, 1962, p. 7.
[64] *Ibid.*, No. 1, 1962, p. 37.
[65] *Ibid.*, No. 11, 1962, p. 30.
[66] *Ibid.*, p. 13.

objective of the Patriarchate is not to transform the non-Orthodox into members of the Orthodox Church as had been its dreams in 1948,[67] but rather to cooperate with them. The Patriarchate is no longer an isolationist as the Orthodox Church had been prior to the Revolution. It is making use of diplomatic means in its pursuit of peaceful coexistence with other religions.

The Patriarchate's sphere widened internationally because the leaders in the Kremlin apparently realized that their international drive for world conquest could best be accomplished by developing internal stability and, furthermore, that Christianity is long-lived and that the Church has avenues of influence which the Kremlin does not have but needs.

From 1948 to 1960 the Church's influence began to widen into international circles. The depth and intensity of its participation in the peace movement, through world-wide conferences with other churches, are increasing. Some of the by-products are obvious by the constant flow of visitors to and from the Patriarchate and the number of greetings exchanged on various occasions. Not only were Orthodox world leaders involved in the above exchange but so were Protestant, Coptic, Old Catholic, and Moslem leaders.

The Patriarchate's participation in the international peace movement has borne fruit; through the controversial peace movement it has succeeded in fragmenting previous Orthodox alliances centered around Patriarch Athenagoras of Constantinople. As early as 1949, a full issue of the *Zhurnal* was devoted to breaking up this honorary alliance in an open effort to get all Slavic support for the Moscow Patriarchate.[68] The Patriarchate has been successful in rallying this Slavic support, and through its participation in the ecumenical movement it has fragmented traditional cleavages. Through its attention to the peace movement it has gained the support of the religious leaders mentioned earlier. By its activities it has also influenced the Roman Catholic Church to talk about unity with those outside the Iron Curtain.

The policies of both the Church and the Kremlin are coordinated but are not identical because of ideological-doctrinal differences, and, even though there is cooperation, charges of heresy have never been brought against the Patriarchal Church. This status quo seems to be in existence since the membership of the Church is not small; neither is the loyalty of the party member shallow.

It is conjectured that before the peace movement ends the Patriarchate will expand its ecumenical activities in search of unity. This is

[67] This is illustrated in the two volumes of the *Dejaniia* published in 1949.
[68] *Zhurnal*, No. 12, 1949, pp. 26–28.

based on the fact that key personnel of the movement are being replaced and their number is being increased. Bishop Nikodim has replaced Metropolitan Nikolai. V. Kuroedov has replaced G. G. Karpov. The chancery and the *Zhurnal* are under their supervision, as is the External Affairs Department of the Church. These men have been brought up and educated under the "new regime," and are the first important ones to replace the men trained and educated during the "old" or Czarist regime.

The scope of their international activities is reflected in at least two areas: in sections of the Zhurnal entitled "In Defense of Peace," to which 31 articles were dedicated in 1963; and the section on "Ecumenical Problems and Questions of Christian Unity," which contained 29 articles. In 1964, the section on peace had 46 articles and the retitled section "Questions of Christian Unity" had 31 articles.

The next few years should begin a new period in the history of the Church. The Church will probably be working more on an international level, and it is possible that Alexei's period will become known as the bridge from one type of Church influence to another. It is regretful that United States news media keep us so poorly informed on the activities of the Russian Orthodox Church in the U.S.S.R. They treat its position much more lightly than does the Kremlin.

CHAPTER VI

National Church Sphere Narrows

As the church leaders in the U.S.S.R. became more active and prominent in international circles, it appears that their national sphere of influence was ebbing. It is difficult to measure the intensity of religious belief in Russia; but upon examination an image of the Church can be seen emerging in the areas of theological education, religious publications, and anti-religious drives. The area of theological education will be studied first.

Theological education. The history of the Russian Orthodox Church attitude toward education is part of the larger history of the State's attitude toward itself. The State was always deeply suspicious of a liberal education. Conservatism prevailed. The courses were so rigidly structured that the student was not encouraged to question whether he wanted to be a Christian and a true son of the State. The Church was duty bound to control the emotional tenor of the citizen so that he would not enter the social sphere of interaction without root or seed. It endeavored to convey the central theme that it was unnatural to separate the educational processes from religious practice, and it stressed that the Church and the State are absolutely necessary for this. Both of these institutions subscribed to the teachings of the early Church Fathers who stressed that the school should relate education under the primacy of the process in which faith was considered a higher gift than intelligence. Neither educational system left room for a modification. If the philosophy of either educational system in Russia during the Czarist period were to be recast, it could be seen that they stressed ideal obedience. No other view was acceptable. As a result, it put the citizen on trial and his deportment and conduct were central to his being a good or poor citizen and a true or false child of God. Intellect and faith were not placed on an equal footing. In the Czarist period of history, it was the "all" of the State, and the "all" of the Church, and finally the "nothingness" of man. This attitude is well illustrated by Nadejda Gorodetzky in *The Humiliated Christ in Modern Russian Thought*.[1]

The analysis of publications indicates that a free press did not exist in Russia under the Czars in contrast to most European countries where censorship was generally abolished in the course of the nineteenth century. The press in Russia was declared free in 1905 by Imperial decree; however, the decree became a dead letter.[2]

The chief forms of self-expression were works of fiction; consequently, literature acquired an importance in Russia which it had long lost in other European countries. The works of Gogol, Tolstoy, Turgenev, and Dostoevsky clearly express self-examination as the main theme. This was the literature offered to those limited few who could read. The complete censorship of all printed material and the lack of mass media as it is known today, radio, television, movies, etc., along with the very high illiteracy rate that prevailed, gave enormous power to the "public speaker."

The clergy were unique because they were one of the few groups who were permitted to speak to the masses. Free public discussions were as a rule prohibited even in the Duma, the legislative body. It was a common practice for clergy in the villages to read the newspaper and other literature and to interpret its content to their parishioners. These sessions were called *chitanki*.[3]

In the schools, religion was a definite part of the mandatory curricula, and ikons were found there as well as in all public buildings. This was a constant reminder that the Church and State were in concerted harmony and that the citizen was subject to both of these institutions.

The theological seminaries were harnessed to pull their share. Their essential purpose was preparing young men for the religious vocation rather than what we commonly call learning. The formal education was marked by a union of general and religious education; all textbooks were censored.

A candidate for the priesthood attended four years of *dukhovnoe uchilische*[4] where the course of study was centered on general education; this was his primary school. He then attended the seminary for six years, four of these years being spent in general studies and the

[1] Nadejda Gorodetzky, *The Humiliated Christ in Modern Russian Thought* (New York: The Macmillan Company, 1938).
[2] J. B. Bury, *A History of the Freedom of Thought* (New York: Henry Holt and Company, 1913), p. 224.
[3] Readings.
[4] Theological primary schools.

last two years concentrated on theological subjects. If he were an outstanding student and in the upper tenth of his class, he could go to the academy for four additional years. Bishops, city deans, and city clergy were usually academy graduates.

Most of the graduates of the theological seminaries in Czarist times were around twenty years old. They were generally about eight when they began their formal education. Their school years extended at least ten years.

With the overthrow of the Czarist regime and seizure of power by the Communists in 1917 the theological seminaries rapidly phased out. The last classes were graduated from the seminaries in the spring of 1918, and the properties of the seminaries were soon confiscated, including their printing presses, and they were closed.

In September, 1918, in Leningrad, a Pastors School was opened. The rector was Archpriest Nicholas Chukov (later Metropolitan Gregori of Leningrad). It was in operation for three years and graduated one class of twenty-three.[5]

Private study classes with bishops and some courses for ordained priests were inaugurated in 1922. However, they were closed within a short time and no course of study was available in the U.S.S.R. for the training of clergy and theologians.

After the registration of the Moscow Patriarchate with the Soviet government in July, 1927, a request was made to receive permission to open a theological institute in Leningrad. Although permission was granted by the Soviets, the institute did not open because "no adequate buildings or professional staff was available."[6] This condition continued until World War II.

At the conference with Stalin on September 4, 1943, a request was again made for permission to open seminaries. Permission was granted. In the next four years, eight seminaries and two academies or graduate schools were opened.

SEMINARIES

Moscow	1944	Lutsk	1946
Odessa	1945	Stavropol	1946
Leningrad	1946	Kiev	1947
Zhirovitzi-Minsk	1946	Saratov	1947

ACADEMIES—GRADUATE SCHOOLS

Moscow	1944	Leningrad	1946

[5] *Zhurnal*, No. 10, 1946, p. 10.
[6] *Ibid.*, p. 11.

Prior to the 1917 Revolution there were 4 academies, 57 seminaries, and 185 theological primary schools in Czarist Russia.

Gregori, Metropolitan of Leningrad, who as Father N. Chukov had headed the short-lived Pastors School in Leningrad in 1918, was entrusted with the task of organizing the new theological program.

The purposes of the theological schools are stated in *The Russian Orthodox Church: Organization, Situation and Activity:*

> The priest's mission in the Church is a great and responsible one, it is the continuation of Christ's work of saving that which was lost (Matt. 18:11). St. Paul enjoins the priest to be an example to the believers, in words, in conversation, in charity, in faith, in purity (1 Tim. 4:12). That is why the training of priests has always been the object of special care on the part of higher Church authorities.
>
> The main task of secondary and higher theological educational institutions is the training of educated and enthusiastic clerics of the Orthodox Church—priests by vocation, able to awaken the moral forces in man and thus contribute to the inner strengthening and prosperity of the Church.[7]

Metropolitan Gregori outlined the proposed plan, stressing the more practical courses as the central core of the curriculum over the theoretical,

> . . . . in view of the fact that the future students of our schools will be much older, a three-year theological course should be sufficient while in the diocese a two-year theological pastoral course should suffice.[8]

At the seminaries no fees were levied against the student; in fact, stipends were given to those who were accepted. An "A" student received 200 rubles per month during his first two years and 300 rubles during his last year at the seminary. He received 400 rubles while doing graduate work. A "B" student received 150, 250, and 300 rubles on the same scale as above; a "C" student received 100, 200, and 250.[9] These scholarships were received after each semester.

The following amounts were disbursed from the Scholarship Fund[10] in 1947: March, 27,950 rubles; April, 27,855 rubles; May, 26,300 rubles; June, 21,450 rubles; Total, 103,555 rubles. An additional 20,000 rubles were given from the Rector's Fund during this period.[11]

---

[7] *The Russian Orthodox Church: Organization, Situation and Activity* p. 103.
[8] *Zhurnal*, No. 3, 1943, p. 22.
[9] *Ibid.*, No. 7, 1947, p. 27.
[10] *Ibid.*, p. 26.
[11] *Ibid.*, p. 27.

In 1952 Patriarch Alexei created three other funds[12] at the Moscow Theological Schools to encourage excellent written work. These were called the Holy Trinity Lavra Fund, the Patriarch Philaret Fund, and the Patriarch Sergei Fund. The amounts that were to be given were not stated, but reference is made that the outstanding students were to receive a 25 percent to 50 percent increase in their scholarships.

In *Patriarch Sergei i ego dukhovnoe nasledstvo*[13] the experiences of the early years following the opening of the seminaries are recorded. It was found that students were poorly equipped for their studies, especially from the spiritual standpoint, and were generally intellectually immature. Lectures were replaced by lessons and quite a few cases of moral unsuitability were reported. Subsequently, more careful screening of students and a strict entrance examination were introduced.

The first theological school was opened in Moscow on June 14, 1944, with ceremonies headed by Patriarch Alexei.[14] Thirteen months later, theological courses were offered in Odessa. The building the school occupied was very small, consisting of fourteen rooms on the second floor.[15] The Leningrad Seminary and Academy opened on October 14, 1946.[16] These were among the first schools opened, and they are possibly the only three still open today in view of the fact that nothing specific regarding their closing is stated in the *Zhurnal*. No reference regarding any but these three schools can any longer be found in the *Zhurnal*.

At no time did the total enrollment of any of these seminaries and academies number over 200 students, and it is doubtful whether the total enrollment of all eight institutions ever numbered over 1000 in any given year. The ratio of instructors to students was very high. For example, when the Moscow Seminary accepted seventy-four students in 1945, its staff consisted of fifteen members with three members of the staff holding the rank of professor.[17]

In 1946, when the Leningrad schools opened, they accepted seventy-four students with room in the dormitories for forty students. Its staff had ten members, three of whom held the rank of professor. Its library was estimated at ten thousand volumes.[18]

The Kiev Seminary accepted eleven students when it opened its doors on February 18, 1947.[19]

[12] *The Russian Orthodox Church: Organization, . . Situation and Activity, . ,* p. 117.
[13] *Patriarch Sergei, op. cit.,* pp. 383–394.
[14] *Zhurnal,* No. 7, 1944, p. 10.
[15] *Ibid.,* p. 21.
[16] *Ibid.,* No. 10, 1946, p. 6.
[17] *Ibid.,* No. 11, 1945, pp. 22–23.
[18] *Ibid.,* No. 10, 1946, p. 12.
[19] *Ibid.,* No. 6, 1947, p. 6.

In 1947 the Moscow Seminary held its first graduation. It graduated eighteen from the original class of seventy-four, eight of these planned to be ordained, eight were to enter the academy, and two were undecided as to their plans.[20]

Apparently the number of students at the theological schools outside of Leningrad and Moscow was very small because seldom is reference made to the number of applicants or graduates. For example, the seminary at Lutsk graduated a class in 1948, but the number of graduates is not indicated.[21] However, the July 1950 issue of the *Zhurnal* states on page 35 that there were sixteen graduates that year.

From all evidence available, it appears that the Patriarchate had a difficult time with its schools even in the early stage right after the concordat. Problems of housing and restriction of travel made things even more difficult, and a new approach was made to try to overcome the pressing limitations. In 1948 local district schools of short duration were put into operation "for those not having enough theological qualifications for ordination."[22] These short courses had the approval of Patriarch Alexei. At Pinsk, twenty-seven men participated in a short course, four of whom had already been ordained as deacons. The course began on May 18 and ended on June 4, 1948.[23] Other references to the short courses can be found in the *Zhurnal*. These short courses were fairly common in each diocese; similar short courses are mentioned also at Vinnitsa and Ulyanovsk.[24] Ulyanovsk is where the central administration was located during the early part of the war.[25]

Correspondence courses[26] were instituted in 1948. Evidently even the short courses presented the problem of housing and transportation. Between 1948 and 1955 it is estimated that 100 completed the basic course and ten completed the course from the academy. According to the *Zhurnal,* the correspondence students gathered at the school for ten days, three times a year, for examination and consultation. Four hundred clergymen were taking these courses in 1955.

In 1948 the theological seminary and academy at Moscow was moved to Zagorsk about fifty miles from Moscow. No statistical information on enrollment or on the number of graduates is given in 1949. Reference to the enrollment states that as many applied as in the previous years. In 1950 the number of applicants was given as 120, out of which forty-three were accepted.[27]

This same year the first graduating class from the Kiev Seminary

[20] *Ibid.*, No. 7, 1947, p. 36.
[21] *Ibid.*, No. 9, 1946, p. 69.
[22] *Ibid.*, No. 7, 1948, p. 69.
[23] *Ibid.*, p. 70.
[24] *Ibid.*, No. 12, 1949, p. 59.
[25] *Ibid.*, No. 3, 1950, p. 62.
[26] *Ibid.*, No. 12, 1955, pp. 28–29.
[27] *Ibid.*, No. 1, 1950, p. 28.

is mentioned. No number is given. The reference made is that all students are doing well.[28] Figures are given for the Moscow and Leningrad institutions. Moscow Seminary was graduating thirty-eight; fourteen were to continue their studies at the academy and twenty were to be ordained parish priests.[29] The total student body at the Moscow institutions was 196, and of this number thirty-seven were graduate students.[30] Leningrad records twenty-one graduates for 1950; seven from the academy and fourteen from the seminary; the total enrollment was 172.[31] This is the last year that specific figures are given regarding student enrollment or graduation.

After 1950, whenever reference is made to seminaries in the *Zhurnal,* it is stated that the applicants are better prepared for their studies, but no details on enrollment are given. The notations indicate that many if not all graduates are being ordained. It is impossible to establish the number of students studying at theological institutions nor is it possible to establish the number graduating. Those figures which are given are in round figures. Other information concerning students, as names of graduates, etc., is lacking. For example, in 1952, we find that "thirty students were accepted at the seminary and thirty at the academy at Leningrad . . . this corresponds to the space available."[32] In 1954 reference can be found concerning the Moscow Seminary. It is stated that, following entrance examinations, forty were accepted at this institution.[33]

Even though students from abroad were to be studying at the seminaries in 1959, the sphere of theological education appeared to be narrowing. The July issue of the *Zhurnal* mentions only the seminaries at Moscow, Leningrad, Odessa, Minsk, Lutsk, and Stavropol or six out of the original eight. One year later, reference in the *Zhurnal* can be found to only five seminaries: Moscow, Leningrad, Odessa, Minsk, and Lutsk. Studying the issues of 1961 to 1963, it appears that only the Moscow, Leningrad, and Odessa theological schools were still in operation. In view of the anti-religious tenor of the press in the Soviet Union at this time, which will be discussed in this chapter, it is doubtful whether the other schools are still open. This view has been arrived at also by assuming that the *Zhurnal* would have at least made passing reference to graduation or opening exercises at the schools (as usual) if they were still open. Since the editorial policy of the *Zhurnal* appears to have no place for negativism, this view is further substantiated.

[28] *Ibid.,* No. 9, 1950, p. 55.
[29] *Ibid.,* No. 8, 1950, p. 69.
[30] *Ibid.,* No. 1, 1950, p. 28.
[31] *Ibid.,* No. 11, 1950, p. 56.
[32] *Ibid.,* No. 11, 1952, pp. 28–29.
[33] *Ibid.,* No. 11, 1954, p. 66.

Curricula of the theological institutions. The curricula of the theological institutions underwent a change during the years 1944 to 1962. The seminary and academy curricula for 1947 were given in *Patriarch Sergei i ego dukhovnoe nasledstvo.*[34]

SEMINARY CURRICULUM—1947

Freshman Class	*Hours per week*
1. History of the Old Testament	4
2. Catechism	4
3. Rubrics (Ritual)	6
4. Survey of Church History	4
5. Church-Slavonic Language	4
* 6. Russian Language	2*
* 7. Slavonic (Church) Reading	2*
* 8. Governmental Situation in U.S.S.R.	2*
9. Church Singing	4
Total	32

Sophomore Class	*Hours per week*
1. History of the New Testament	4
2. Catechism	4
3. Rubrics (Ritual)	6
4. Russian Church History	4
5. Church Slavonic Language	4
* 6. Russian Language	2*
* 7. Slavonic (Church) Reading	2*
8. Constitutions of U.S.S.R.	2
9. Church Singing	4
Total	32

Junior Class	*Hours per week*
1. Old Testament-Scriptures	4
2. New Testament-Scriptures	4
3. Dogmatic Theology	4
* 4. Fundamental Theology	2*
* 5. Fundamental Psychology	2*
6. Liturgics	2
7. Homiletics	2
8. Practical Guidance for Pastors	2
* 9. History of the Ancient Church	4*

[34] *Patriarch Sergei, op. cit.,* pp. 394–397.

Junior Class (Continued)	*Hours per week*
10. Schismatics and Sectarians	4
11. Church Music	2
12. Greek Language	2
13. Modern Language	2
Total	36

Senior Class	*Hours per week*
1. Old Testament-Scriptures	4
2. New Testament-Scriptures	4
3. Dogmatic Theology	4
4. Moral Theology	4
* 5. Fundamental Theology	2*
6. Comparative Theology	2
7. Liturgics	2
8. Homiletics	2
9. History of the Russian Church	4
10. Schismatics and Sectarians	2
*11. History of Russian Religious Thought	2*
12. Greek Language	2
13. Modern Language	2
Total	36

* Indicates courses removed according to the listing in *The Russian Orthodox Church: Organization, Situation and Activity*, English ed., p. 104; Russian ed., pp. 110, 121.

The courses which are not found in the present curriculum are Fundamental Psychology, History of Russian Religious Thought, Slavonic (Church) Reading, Russian Language, and Governmental Situation. History of the Ancient Church, Schismatics and Sectarians have been included under one heading and entitled Analysis of the Doctrines of the Russian Schism and Sects. Fundamental Theology has been retitled Apologetics.

ACADEMY CURRICULUM—1947

The original curriculum corresponded to the pre-revolutionary academy curriculum.

	Classes and hours per week			
	I	II	III	IV
1. Old Testament—Scriptures	4	4	—	—
2. New Testament—Scriptures	—	—	4	4
3. Dogmatic Theology	2	2	2	—

Classes and hours per week

4. Moral Theology	—	2	2	2
5. Pastoral Theology with Ascetics	—	—	2	—
* 6. Christian Apologetics	—	—	2	2*
7. Liturgics and Hymnology	2	2	—	—
8. Church Archeology in conjunction with the history of Christian Art	—	—	2	—
9. Homiletics in conjunction with the history of church sermons	2	2	—	—
10. History of the Christian Church	4	—	—	—
11. History of the Greco-Eastern, Slavic and Rumanian Church	—	2	—	—
12. History of the Russian Church	—	—	2	—
13. History and Analysis of the Western Confessions	—	—	4	—
14. History and Analysis of the teachings of the Russian sects	2	2	—	—
15. History of Religion	—	—	2	—
*16. History of Russian Religious Thought	2	2	—	—*
17. Patristics and Hagiology	—	2	2	—
*18. Logic	2	—	—	—*
*19. Psychology	4	—	—	—*
*20. History of Philosophy and Metaphysics	—	4	—	—*
*21. Christian Pedagogy (didactics and methods)	—	—	—	2*
22. Canon Law	—	—	—	4
23. Constitution of U.S.S.R.	—	—	—	2
24. Ancient Languages	2	2	2	—
25. Modern Languages	2	2	2	—
Total	28	28	28	16

* Indicates courses which have been removed from the present curriculum: Christian Apologetics, History of Russian Religious Thought, Logic, Psychology, History of Philosophy and Metaphysics, and Christian Pedagogy (didactics and methods).

Since none of the publications of the Moscow Patriarchate give full details regarding the course of study, it is difficult to judge the breadth or depth of the academic program. It can be seen that in the seminaries a choice of either English, German, or French was added and the required number of subjects was lowered from twenty-eight to twenty-three. In the academies, it appears that Greek and Latin were added with either English, German, or French as optional languages and the number of required subjects was lowered from twenty-five to twenty-one.

Languages were added to the course of study. Several subjects were dropped. In the original listing it can be seen that the student was required to take two hours a week of Basic Psychology and of the History of Russian Religious Thought. These were dropped along with the History of Metaphysics, Logic, Pastoral Pedagogy, and Christian Apologetics. With the elimination of these subjects, the course of study would appear to be deficient in the area of current human behavior. These subjects would appear to be essential to the future priest if he wished to come to grips with the contemporary society. The curriculum underwent this fundamental and significant change as it adapted itself to the limiting conditions of Soviet society. This change indicates that the education of the clergy, probably training is more correct, has become narrower and shallower. It has relegated intellectual learning to a much lower rung than ritual and belief.

Theological education is also hampered by the dearth of theological textbooks. Sources that are available in seminary libraries are not printed but typewritten. These are the typewritten lecture notes, and it is unusual to find the works of one seminary in another seminary library. They seem to be kept only in the library of the school where they are given. A sharing or exchange of these textbooks is not usual. The contents of these books are closely related and based on earlier pre-Revolution works. The author acknowledges the theologians whose works he has used. It is uncommon to find listed in the bibliography any book printed after 1917 which discusses western theological thought. It would seem that theological thought was frozen in 1917. The material on dogmatics thawed out enough to have devoted two pages to religion and science.[35]

The Kremlin apparently does not encourage theological education but only tolerates theological technicians at best. The curriculum leaves little room for research and individual thought. In 1960 the *Zhurnal*[36] indicated the subjects selected for dissertations at the academy. Here are a few titles: in the area of the Old Testament—*The Messianic Prophesy of the Book of Genesis, The Teaching of the Old Testament Regarding the Immortal Soul of Man;* in the New Testament area—*Witnessing of St. Paul of His Being Sent from God, Eschatology of St. Paul According to His First Epistle to the Corinthians;* in the area of Dogmatic Theology—*The Dogma of Salvation in Russian Theological Literature in the Past Fifty Years,* and *Teachings Regarding Salvation Based Upon the Twelve Feast Days in the Lenten and Bright Triod and Octoech.* Quite a few dissertation titles indicate a historical study concerning the conflict between Catholicism

[35] A. Johansen, *Theological Study in the Russian and Bulgarian Orthodox Churches under Communist Rule* (London: The Faith Press, 1963).
[36] *Zhurnal,* No. 4, 1960, pp. 41–46.

and Orthodoxy and about the Autocephalous Orthodox Churches. It appears from the titles that the dissertations are not concerned with social welfare problems in contemporary society but rather with historical material related to theology. None of the titles listed indicates a social science orientated research.

Man is influenced by his society. Yet it appears that the graduates of the theological schools in the U.S.S.R. will not have much impact upon the Soviet way of life because they are too few in number and their education is not structured to give them insight into the minds of men. The social and natural sciences are not part of their formal education. Once out in the field, they are further inhibited by not having the freedom to truly reach their people through educational or social organizations.

The Communist way of life has had an impact on the theological education, and the schools have had to adapt themselves. The schools are unable to resist the anti-religious Communist influence because they are dependent upon the State for their continued existence. They have to submit to their reference group which dominates their program and behavior as well as their inner and outer social direction. The schools have accommodated themselves; however, the Communists still persist in their avowed conflict with religious ideology. The number of graduates is very small; probably less than a hundred graduate each year. Contrast this figure with the following statement:

> In making its application, the Church (Patriarchate) lists 30,-000 priests and 73 bishoprics inside the U.S.S.R. There are 20,-000 parishes and 40 monasteries. The eight theological schools maintained by the Church include two academies and six seminaries. It does not mention the number of members. The Russian Orthodox Church traditionally has not published its membership.[37]

It is improbable that the statement cited above can be readily accepted in view of what the *Zhurnal* reflects in its pages.

Religious publications. Very little has been printed in the Soviet Union which may be classified as religious publications. There is the official monthly journal of the Patriarchate, the annual calendar (rubrics), a few historical books, the liturgical service books and a book which describes the Church. The Patriarchate does not publish any religious tracts, pamphlets or books concerning religion, the Christian faith or the truth of the Bible. Neither does it print, mimeograph or sponsor in any way any circulars, bulletins, leaflets, or invi-

[37] *Press Release*, World Council of Churches, April 27, 1961.

tations to Church services. This is strictly forbidden by Article 124 of the Soviet Constitution.

Zhurnal Moskovskoi Patriarchii[38] has been the official monthly journal since September 12, 1943. The first issue stated its purpose on page 1:

The *Zhurnal Moskovskoi Patriarchii* will contain official decisions of the Patriarch on church matters, his missals, decisions and the appointments of the Patriarch and the Holy Synod, the patriotic activities of the Patriarch and other churchmen, articles of a theological nature, calendar references and other notations concerning the life of the Church . . .

From 1943 until 1963 the *Zhurnal* has not deviated from its original plan; however, the accounts of its patriotic activities have far overshadowed the other parts of the purpose. This is particularly true of the work being done in the international sphere: relationship with the non-Orthodox, the fight for peace, and the travels abroad by its representatives. Articles of a historical nature centered around the saints and the fathers appear often. On the other hand, the *Zhurnal* is deficient on "notations concerning the life of the church," in particular ordinations, assignments, general depositions of clergy, and general current events beyond any one diocese and bishop.

The *Zhurnal* has expanded in size and scope since its first issue in 1943. It first consisted of twenty pages, had expanded to about sixty in 1955, continued to expand, and at present has up to eighty pages. The content never reflects in the slightest any unfavorable attitude or opinion which could be considered a criticism of the government. In international matters the *Zhurnal* mirrors the sentiments of the government on world affairs. There is every reason to believe that it is censored and has a limited circulation.

By the references which are lacking in the *Zhurnal*, we can construe that propagation of the faith is absent in the Soviet Union as proscribed by Article 124 of the 1936 Constitution. No reference can be found to religious radio broadcasts, evangelism, missionary activities, prayer circles or other methods used in reaching the public, outside of the worship service in the church building. Neither can reference be found in the *Zhurnal* which conveys a religious concern for the social welfare of the believers. The Church cannot carry on any welfare or philanthropic work even among its members in distress.[39] Such organizations as homes for the aged, orphanages, hospitals, relief for the needy and sick, Ladies' Aid, Men's Brotherhoods, Youth Groups, etc., are all prohibited.

[38] *Journal of the Moscow Patriarchate.*
[39] See Appendix C.

All of the restrictions listed in the Forty-eight Paragraphs of 1945 and as amended in 1961 are apparently adhered to by fulfilling the letter of the law. The content of the *Zhurnal* in the years of its publication gives the image of a Church which, at best, is tolerated and amenable to the control of the Soviet State; which in turn is under the immediate direction of the Communist Party in all spheres of its economic, social, and political life.

Besides the *Zhurnal,* the next most widely circulated publication is the *Pravoslavnij tzerkovnij kalendar'*[40] printed since 1944. At first, it was printed on newsprint but the quality of paper has improved in the last ten years. This *Kalendar* consists of approximately eighty pages and follows a set form each year. It contains a picture of the Patriarch, a liturgical calendar for the year, photos of the sacred shrines, about ten pages listing the saints and their feast days, a listing of the ikons of the Theotokos and their feast days, a listing of important national holidays and events such as the day of Lenin's death, etc. The remaining ten pages are devoted to general guidance concerning the divine services of the feast days, the epistle and gospel readings for these days and liturgical changes for movable feast days.

The most beautifully illustrated book published by the Patriarchate was *Pravda o religii v Rossii* in 1942.[41] It contains 450 pages printed in red and black. The main theme is the desecration of the religious monuments by the Nazis and how helpful the Soviets have been to the Patriarchate. It contains many mounted photos and the cover and title pages are imprinted in gold. The paper is of excellent quality.

In 1947 the Patriarchate printed *Patriarch Sergei i ego dukhovnoe nasledstvo,*[42] consisting of over four hundred pages of compliments to Patriarch Sergei and the State. A sketch is given of his life, his publications and articles, his burial service, and most of all his legacy to the Church in the U.S.S.R.

Several other books were printed. Those dealing with peace were more numerous. In 1947, 1954, and 1957, all the speeches, directives, and appeals made by Patriarch Alexei and Metropolitan Nikolai were put into book form. Alexei's volumes totaled about 400 pages, while Nikolai's totaled about 1000 pages in Volumes I, III, and IV. Evidently, a second volume was published between 1947 and 1954 but it could not be located. Reprints of their speeches have been made into several languages. The English language edition, entitled *The Russian Orthodox Church in the Fight for Peace,* was released in 1950. About four volumes carrying some of Nikolai's speeches on peace have been published in English.

[40] *The Orthodox Church Calendar.*
[41] *The Truth About Religion in Russia.*
[42] *Patriarch Sergei and His Spiritual Legacy.*

Many meetings were held between July 8 and 18, 1948, when the Patriarchate invited all the world leaders of Orthodoxy to the 500th anniversary of the autocephaly of the Russian Orthodox Church. The notes were printed in two thick volumes *Dejaniia soveschaniia glav i predstavitelei avtokefal'nikh pravoslavnikh tzerkvei.*[43] These books extol the State and call for the Orthodox Churches of the world to unite under the leadership of the Patriarch of Moscow. The Orthodox leaders condemned the Pope's attitude toward the Nazis and Fascists.

The Patriarchate has released photo-offset books which are necessary for the performance of ritual: *Biblia, Trebnik, Molitvoslov,* and *Sluzhebnik.* These books are copies of those printed prior to the revolution, and material not pertinent to the present society was deleted with blanks left in the text.

The most recent publication is *The Russian Orthodox Church: Organization, Situation, and Activity,* which has been printed in Russian, English, German, French, Italian, Spanish, and Arabic. The Russian edition is dated 1958. The English edition is undated. The book is amply illustrated with about one hundred pages of photographs. The text takes an equal amount of pages. The State is exalted. The section on the "Structure and Administration of the Russian Church" consists of eleven pages, three of which contain photographs. The section on "The Russian Orthodox Church in the Struggle for Peace" has twenty pages, three of them containing photographs.

This paucity of religious books and periodicals, and the abundance of anti-religious books, articles, and pamphlets, show that the law, Article 124 in the Soviet Constitution, "Freedom of religious worship and freedom of anti-religious propaganda is recognized for all citizens," is strictly adhered to. Negatively, it means there is no freedom for religious propaganda.

Anti-religious press and publications. Not reflected in the *Zhurnal* are the attacks against religion which continue in the Soviet press. At times, non-Orthodox groups are singled out; then, the Orthodox group is belittled; then religion in general is attacked. The anti-religious propaganda endeavors to stress that science and religion are incompatible and that communism is based on scientific knowledge; therefore, it cannot have anything in common with religion because religion is unscientific and unverifiable, and thus a conflicting ideology.

Our system of society fosters the development and strengthening of a scientific world outlook and the liberation of Soviet citizens from religious persuasions. . . . The entire system of communism is scientific and hence anti-religious, for science is the opposite of religion. . . . One cannot be a progressive, fully-

---

[43] *The Acts and Conferences of Heads and Representatives of the Autocephalous Orthodox Churches.*

aware fighter for communism . . . if he believes in a life after death, just as it is impossible to be a consistent champion of science, if one is not free of scientific anti-religious convictions.[44]

The individual stands at the center of the Western democratic theory of politics. The Soviet theory puts the State in the pivotal position. Life, liberty, and the pursuit of happiness are exact opposites of Hegelian concepts of citizenship, of self-sacrifice, duty, and discipline. In his philosophy the State is moral life, it is the absolute idea. Consequently, freedom of religion or religious expressions as we know them can not exist. Power has become the vital principle of the Soviet State; it is not interested in what an individual desires, but that he have total dedication. Herein lies the nature of the Soviet State. It denies the majority power. The individual lives for Soviet society; Soviet society becomes the spiritual and moral fact in itself. The individual must therefore conceive of life as a duty to the State. He lives in society in behalf of the State, and therefore all justice is only through the State. The common man and the institutions are thus kept under control and often in subjection. Opponents are liquidated or muted by this system, and the dignity of man is removed; so are the freedom of press, and the freedom to believe and to propagate one's religious belief.

The Constitution of the Union of Soviet Socialist Republics clearly states its position concerning the right to religious belief in its articles. Article 124 states:

> In order to ensure citizens freedom of conscience, the Church in the U.S.S.R. is separated from the State, and the schools from the Church. Freedom of religious worship and freedom of anti-religious propaganda is recognized for all citizens.[45]

Article 125 states:

> In conformity with the interests of the working people and in order to strengthen the socialist system, the citizens of the U.S.S.R. are guaranteed by law:
>
> a) freedom of speech;
> b) freedom of the press;
> c) freedom of assembly, including the holding of mass meetings;
> d) freedom of street processions and demonstrations.

The civil rights are ensured by placing at the disposal of the working people and their organizations, printing presses, stocks

[44] *Kulturno prosvetitel'naia rabota*, No. 5, May 1949, pp. 24–30.
[45] Denisov and Kirichenko, *op. cit.*, p. 405.

of paper, public buildings, the streets, communications facilities, and other material requisite for the exercise of these rights.[46]

The Soviet system of government provides sharp contrast to the system that obtains in the United States. This contrast provokes thought on the structure and function of political institutions. State opposition to religion is most noticeable by the fact that all rights are predicated upon whether the action is "to strengthen the socialist system." Because religion, according to Communist philosophy, does not strengthen the social system, it does not enjoy the freedom of public expression. Religion is associated in Soviet minds with potential opposition to the regime; therefore, the Soviet government, supposedly neutral, is against those who profess religion. This opposition has intensified.

The 1918 and 1924 Constitutions provided: "Freedom of religious and anti-religious propaganda is recognized for all citizens."

The 1936 Constitution read: "Freedom of religious worship" is permitted and "freedom of anti-religious propaganda is recognized for all citizens." Consequently, it implies that religious propagandistic and missionary work are not permitted. In reality such activities are considered harmful, are violations of the laws on freedom of conscience and are prosecuted in accordance with criminal and civil laws.[47]

The Statutes of the Communist Party of the Soviet State, adopted by the Twenty-second Party Congress in 1961, provide under the title "Party Members, their Duties and Rights" " (d) . . . to combat resolutely . . . religious prejudices and their survivals of the past, to observe the rules of Communist morality and to place public interests above personal ones."[48] The anti-religious activities of the Party sanctioned by the State are to be found in articles which appear in special sections of: *Agitator, Politicheskoe samoobrazovanie (Political Self Education)*, *Voprosy istorii (Historical Questions-Problems)*, *Nauka i Zhisn (Science and Life)* *Znanie sila (Knowledge is Power)*, *Priroda (Nature)*, *Zdorov'e (Health)*, *Rabotnitza (Working Woman)*, *Krest'ianka (Peasant Woman)*, *Smena (Change)*, and in related publications in the republics.

The Communist Party has intensified its fight against religion by naming special committees to conduct the anti-religious work. In addition, learned journals, the daily papers, radio, television, public movies, and public education are used as channels for this work. These are explicitly denied believers and their associations.

[46] *Ibid.*
[47] See Appendix B. "Infringement of the Regulations for the Separation of Church and State."
[48] *Current Digest of the Soviet Press,* Vol. 13, No. 47, Dec. 20, 1961.

Izvestia (daily organ of the government) has a circulation of 4,100,-000, and *Pravda* (daily organ of the Central Committee of the Communist Party of the Soviet Union has a circulation of 6,000,000.[49])

Throughout the 146 articles of the Constitution it is clearly evident that the power lies in the hands of the Communists who rule the Soviet Union. Article 146 states:

> The Constitution of the U.S.S.R. may be amended only by decision of the Supreme Soviet of the U.S.S.R. adopted by a majority of not less than two-thirds of the vote in each of its Chambers.

Obviously only Communists who are avowed atheists and promoters of anti-religious propaganda may be seated in the Supreme Soviet.

A very significant role has always been assigned to the press in the area of anti-religious propaganda. Lenin felt that the paper was a collective organizer.

> The periodical and non-periodical press and all publishing enterprises must be entirely subordinated to the Central Committee of the Party, irrespective of whether the party as a whole is legal or illegal at the given moment; publishing enterprises must not be permitted to abuse their autonomy by pursuing a policy that is not entirely the party policy.[50]

Stalin made it crystal clear that there is no freedom of the press for the bourgeoisie.

> If it is freedom of the press for the bourgeoisie then it (freedom of the press) does not exist and will not exist here as long as the dictatorship of the proletariat is in power. . . . We have never pledged ourselves to grant freedom of the press to all classes, to make all classes happy.[51]

Khrushchev thought of the press as the Party's main ideological weapon.

> The press is our main ideological weapon. It is called upon to rout the enemies of the working class. . . . Just as an army cannot fight without weapons, so the Party cannot successfully carry out its ideological work without such a sharp and militant weapon

---

[49] Anthony Buzek. *How the Communist Press Works* (London: Pall Mall Press, 1964), p. 271.

[50] Lenin, "Conditions of Affiliation to the Communist International," 1920, Vol. of *Selected Works* (New York: International Publishers, 1943), p. 204.

[51] Stalin, "Interview with Foreign Workers Delegation," November 5, 1927, Vol. I of *Leninism* (Moscow: Cooperation Publishing Society of Foreign Workers, 1934), pp. 403–404.

as the press in *reliable* hands.[52] They must be in the hands of the workers who are most faithful, most reliable, politically staunch and loyal to our cause.[53]

The Great Soviet Encyclopedia notes that the Church exists legally in the U.S.S.R.; however, it points out in the final paragraph:

The Communist Party considers religion as an ideology, having nothing in common with science, and therefore it cannot remain neutral. . . . The Party . . . considers it necessary to conduct profound systematic scientific-atheistic propaganda.[54]

In reality, the persecution of the Church and an anti-religious press continue in the U.S.S.R. They come in waves of emphasis and de-emphasis. During the Second World War, the anti-religious press was silenced. For a short time after 1946, very little anti-religious propaganda appeared. In fact, *Pravda* and *Izvestia* often carried articles by churchmen of the Orthodox Church which showed or implied the Church's loyalty to the State. The *Zhurnal* reflected this and in its January issue it carried a statement concerning freedom of conscience.

On the 10th of February our great united multinational Soviet people will . . . tell who of the candidates of the block of Communists are worthy to become members of the Supreme Soviet of the U.S.S.R. . . . Inspired priests will step forth from the amvon and will bless their spiritual children to hasten forth from the Church to the ballot boxes. They will bless them to give their vote to the candidates of the block of Communists. . . . Why? Firstly, because the ministers of the Church as well as all her members are at one with and inseparable from their own people. Secondly, because in the entire world there are no conditions more favorable for the flourishing of the Holy Church of Christ than those which are found in the soviet land. All the faithful know that the candidates of this block will preserve their conditions and will even improve them, if this is possible.

Indeed, where, in what country is the Church as free from the fetters of the State and from political intrigues, where does the State, while demanding nothing from the Church, surround her with such attention? . . . (Nowhere else on) earth are there and can there be better relations (between Church and State) than

[52] Underlined in original.
[53] Khrushchev, "For a Close Tie of the Literature and Art with the Life of the People," *Kommunist*, No. 12, 1957, p. 23.
[54] *Pravda*, Nov. 11, 1954, No. 315, p. 2, as quoted in *Bol'shaiia sovetskaia entsiklopedia*, Vol. 36, 2d ed., Gosudarstvenoe Nauchnoe Izdatel'stvo, 1955, p. 339.

those relations which obtain in our country. . . . This is why all the Orthodox Russian people will joyously give their votes to the candidates of the block of Communists.[55]

This reflective press continued in 1948 and 1949. For example, long condemnatory articles against the Vatican appeared both in the State and Church presses. In February, *the Bolshevik,*[56] *Sovetskaia pedagogika,*[57] and *Literaturnaia gazeta*[58] condemned the Vatican. In August the *Zhurnal* carried an article calling for unity of the Christian world but not through the Roman Catholic Church's strivings nor through the Protestant Ecumenical movement but by returning to the teachings of the ancient indivisible church—the Orthodox Church.[59] When the government granted the Patriarchate permission to hold the meeting of all Orthodox leaders in 1948 in Zagorsk, the proceedings of the meetings were recorded in two volumes, where among other things, the Vatican was condemned.[60]

※ In reviewing Soviet publications for the years 1948 to 1962, certain patterns emerge. In the early period after the war, the approach in fighting religion was based upon enlightenment and reason. The sects were attacked; the Orthodox Church as such was still immune from public attack. The September, 1949, issue of *Literaturnaia gazeta* contained an article concerning the fanaticism of a man who preached in spite of the fact that registration had been refused him. It said that his children should be taken away from him since he was infecting them.

Belimov founded a sect, but the supreme sect authorities in Moscow refused to acknowledge it because of several evidences of outright fanaticism which entered into Belimov's mad dogmatics.[61]

This also shows one example of how complete the control of the Soviet regime has become regarding even the registration of a belief. Not all beliefs are sanctioned; in fact some are outlawed even though they operate in other countries. Such is the case of the Jehovah's

[55] *Zhurnal*, No. 1, 1946, pp. 30–31.
[56] O. Nikitin, "The Vatican—Weapon of Imperialism," *Bolshevik*, February 15, 1948, pp. 73–80.
[57] "The Reactionary Role of the Vatican in Education," *Sovetskaia pedagogika*, February 2, 1949, pp. 82–89.
[58] S. M. Rozenoyer, "The Vatican and Wall Street," *Literaturnaia gazeta*, February 19, 1949.
[59] *Zhurnal*, No. 7, 1948, pp. 68–80.
[60] *Dejania soveshannia* . . . , Vol. I, pp. 95–279; Vol. II, pp. 200–233, 426–430.
[61] Ivan Yegorov, "Kitayevskiye Fakirs," *Literaturnaia gazeta*, September, 1949, p. 2.

Witnesses, who are outlawed and are called an "espionage organization which is in the control of an imperialist power."[62]

As stated earlier, no direct criticism was made on the Patriarchate during this period. The Patriarch was alert to international conditions, and the Soviet press noted it on such occasions.

> Alexei and six others return Yugoslav decorations because of the clearly hostile attitude of the present Yugoslav government to our (Soviet) Union.[63]

The Patriarchate reflected the attitude of the State. When the State was hostile to the government of Yugoslavia, the Patriarchate would also be hostile to the Serbian Orthodox Church in Yugoslavia.

> The comedy of "election" of a Patriarch of the Serbian Orthodox Church has once more demonstrated the rottenness of the Tito Regime, hated by the masses of Yugoslav people . . . the rope will tighten around the traitors' necks.[64]

In 1950 articles began to appear acknowledging that religion would not die of itself in the course of the development of a socialist system. Young Communist League members were especially criticized and told not to be neutral. A question appeared in *Komsomol'skaia pravda:* "Can I marry a believer in church?" The following answer is given. "Such an act, if you perform it, directly violates the Young Communist League statutes. It contradicts Communist ethics and is incompatible with the title Young Communist."[65]

Articles called for more aggressive and better conducted anti-religious propaganda. People were called upon to become more systematic and more serious about their anti-religious work. The need for more literature was stressed, but it was emphasized that no sudden or dictatorial measures should be taken that would offend the religious person.[66] The call for more literature was answered with forty pamphlets totaling 800,000 copies, "pamphlets exposing foreign religiosity and the Catholic Church as an instrument of American imperialism in the propagation of a new world war."[67] Emphasis was continued in explaining the position of religion to young Communists.

[62] *Pravda,* September 6, 1950, p. 4.
[63] *Izvestia,* March 15, 1950, p. 5.
[64] *Literaturnaia gazeta,* August 5, 1950, p. 4.
[65] *Komsomol'skaia pravda,* March 21, 1950, p. 3.
[66] *Nauka i zhisn,* No. 8, August, 1950, p. 48.
[67] *Kultura i zhisn,* January 11, 1951, p. 3.

To believe in God or not to believe in God is not a personal affair of the Young Communist League member since religious concepts are foreign to the communist outlook . . . [they] are obliged to struggle against the remnants of religious prejudices.[68]

The same policy was evident throughout 1952 and 1953. The youth was called upon to enter into a more vigorous struggle against religion, which was referred to as a remnant of the old society and superstitions which remained in the consciousness of the population.

Articles began to appear in 1953 discussing the Church holidays which were celebrated by the people. They said that many people celebrating these holidays did not know their religious significance but merely wanted to "make merry." Many suggestions were given to counteract their influence. The most often repeated thought was to keep the days but call them Sport Day, and activities were suggested to celebrate these days of relaxation.

The pace of anti-religious propaganda was stepped up in 1954 after Stalin's death. A different approach was used from 1954 to 1958, less emotional and more clinical in tone. On November 10, 1954, the Central Committee of the Communist Party stepped forward to decree that there is need to:

. . . eliminate errors in atheistic propaganda. . . . The Party considers profound, systematic-scientific-atheistic propaganda essential, without however, permitting the religious feelings of believers and clergy to be offended.

Khrushchev made this comment which was widely printed.[69] It was further said that neither sensational headlines nor offensive cartoons were to be used.

A sector on the history of religion and atheism was reorganized in the History Institute of the U.S.S.R. Academy of Sciences in 1954.[70] Its purpose was to set up a library. It was to reissue the works of the French eighteenth century enlighteners and materialists, such as Voltaire, Rousseau, Helvitius, Diderot, Holback; the earlier critics and the freethinkers of the sixteenth century, such as Campanella, and Bodin; the atheists of ancient times, such as Democritus, Epicurius, Lauretius, and Lucian; and of the Russian atheists. Some of these anti-religious books were printed in large numbers up to 200,000 copies.[71]

---

[68] *Komsomol'skaia pravda,* April 25, 1951, p. 3.
[69] *Pravda, Trud,* and *Komsomol'skaia pravda,* November 12, 1954; and *Partinaia zhisn,* No. 15, pp. 9–15.
[70] *Vestnik academii nauk,* SSSR, No. 10, 1954, pp. 85–86.
[71] *Sovetskaia kultura,* January 6, 1955, "All-Union Seminar on Scientific-Atheistic Propaganda," p. 2.

A great attempt was made to improve the quality of written materials and lectures. The anti-religious elements continued to call for intensified campaigns in the press and for a complete work on the history of atheism, as they felt it would become a major contribution to scholarship which would have great political value. They stressed that overcoming religious survival was a great and important task which was indissolubly linked with the construction of a new life. Seminars were held for directors and permanent lecturers of the Central Lecture Bureau. These seminars lasting ten days were convened by the collegium of the U.S.S.R. Ministry of Cults. In attendance were eighty representatives from all sixteen capitals of the Union Republics. Lectures were given by academicians. Mention was made at the seminars that fifty new pamphlets were published recently and that new visual aids were also prepared to combat religion.[72]

The teaching methods in public schools on matters of anti-religion were also re-examined. Articles appeared in journals on higher education telling how teachers should integrate anti-religious material in different fields. Examples of how certain named teachers were doing this were given. Social science teachers[73] were especially singled out, and it was pointed out that these teachers should extend their own knowledge of the origin of religion and the role of the churches in non-communist countries. Teachers were told that it was important for them to be active in anti-religious propaganda since it was apparent that there were still parents who evidently were believers and who had a bad influence on their children.

The work was intensified among servicemen, and criticism of the House of Officers was made saying that they neglected their duty in the area of anti-religious propaganda and that this would not be tolerated.[74]

The end of 1955 brought articles which stated that there had been a noticeable improvement in the quality and quantity of anti-religious work.[75] *Pravda* carried an article on page 1, noting that an *Anthology* of Karl Marx and Frederick Engels had been published.[76]

During 1956 and 1957 the usual criticism continued to appear in the Soviet press calling upon the anti-religious propagandist to shake the faith and comparing the present work unfavorably with the zealous lectures of the 1930 era. The press complained about the passivity of the officials in the Young Communist League. For the first time, it was advocated that lectures be extended to reach housewives, invalids,

[72] *Sovetskaia litva,* No. 3, 1955, p. 3.
[73] *Vestnik vysshei shkoli,* No. 3, 1955, pp. 21–22.
[74] *Sovetsky flot,* Editorial, September 6, 1955, p. 1.
[75] *Sovetskaia kultura,* Editorial, August 16, 1955, p. 1.
[76] *Pravda,* November 13, 1955, p. 1.

and older people since this segment of the Soviet population had been neglected. On December 16, 1957, it was suggested in *Izvestia* that the traditional holidays of the Church should be kept but should not have a religious significance. It stressed the need for Harvest Days and the honoring of the best workers. The author, Ivan Tayupa, felt that the people needed holidays as a respite, but he stressed "religion is one thing and a folk ceremony is something else." From this it would seem that much had not been done in this area since the last references to holidays in 1953. The people's need for time honored customs was realized. It was suggested that a substitute form for wedding ceremonies be established. Wedding palaces were set up.

It is significant that the writer also stressed the use of radio in antireligious propaganda. He felt that it was a great mistake to keep the wires silent on this issue.

The Society for the Dissemination of Scientific Knowledge endeavored to use all segments of the population which could contribute to the success of their program. The Moscow Academy of Science began to publish an annual yearbook in 1957 called *Ezhegodnik muzea istorii religii i ateisma.*[77] These annuals are hardbound books, average over four hundred pages and are printed on glossy paper and in a form which shows that they are meant to be added to someone's library to be used as reference books. The *Ezhegodnik,* for each of the years studied, notes that over four hundred articles against religion were published in the U.S.S.R. in various newspapers and magazines in the respective years mentioned. In 1958 the *Annual* attacked religion in general; in 1959 it discussed the problem areas in Marxist-Atheism and reviewed atheistic experiences in the U.S.S.R., Europe and America. The 1960 *Ezhegodnik* criticized Orthodox theology and the Church in general, and it critically reviewed the *Zhurnal.*

Much more literature began to appear in the form of pamphlets in 1958. *Communist* in May, 1958, complained that not enough literature had been published even though it noted later in the article that 106 anti-religious publications were released in 1957 in the U.S.S.R.

In August, 1958, twelve atheistic books were published and widely circulated. Some of these were:

Voprosi religii i ateisma[78]
Materialism i religia[79]
Biblia dlya veruushih i neveruushih[80]

[77] *Annual of the Museum of the History of Religion and Atheism.*
[78] *Questions on Religion and Atheism,* 440 pages, 50,000 copies.
[79] *Materialism and Religion,* 250 pages, 50,000 copies.
[80] *Bible for Believers and Non-Believers,* 10th edition, 150,000 copies.

Ateism, obschestvo i religia[81]
Primirima li nauka i religia?[82]

This list was added to. In November, 1958, the following were published by the Soviet press:

Voprosi istorii, religii i ateisma[83]
Kniga o Biblii[84]
Sushestvuet li bog?[85]

Emphasis Changes in 1959. Names of people connected with religion began to appear, and the stories and incidents told were defamatory in nature. This showed that the Communist doctrinal commitment to destroy religion had in no way been abrogated by the diplomatic rapprochement between the Church and the State; only the terrain and tactics of the battle had been shifted. The Communist concept of the freedom of conscience and the educational campaign seek to discredit the religious ideology by scientific-atheistic argument and to supplant the religious content by neutralizing and replacing it with its own ethics, customs, and ceremonials.

The Soviet press makes it very clear in its articles against religion that "he who is not with us is against us." The outlook upon religion is not merely that it is outmoded, outdated, useless, and obsolete; but that it is a hostile force which must be removed from the Soviet scene. As is evident from the press, a very special place is given in it to show that religion is an opiate and that a deathly struggle has ensued to break this habit of belief in an omnipotent Creator. The press and other mass media in recent years have become more systematic and relentless in their pursuit to eradicate religion from the scene.

Primary concern is for the youth. The State intends to keep them so busy they will not have the time or desire to visit places of worship. It stresses the legal measures which can be taken as means of control—no one under eighteen may join a church and even after he is eighteen it sometimes takes a year or two before he may join because of various restrictions and social pressures. When one finally does break with his youth group, such as the Young Communist League, he is ridiculed even by the press. In *Izvestia*[86] a criticism is leveled against a young man who becomes interested in religion. He is considered immoral, of low repute, and discreditable.

[81] *Atheism, Society and Religion,* 50,000 copies.
[82] *Are Science and Religion Compatible?,* 100,000 copies.
[83] *Questions Regarding History, Religion and Atheism,* 244 pages, published by the Academy of Sciences.
[84] *A Book About the Bible,* 360 pages, 125,000 copies.
[85] *Does God Exist?,* 80 pages, 150,000 copies.
[86] *Izvestia,* October 14, 1960, p. 6.

When, on the other hand, some one rejects religion, as was the case of a priest, Alexander Osipov, the press has praise and congratulations to offer. Osipov's criticism of the Church got full coverage.[87] He called the Church anti-democratic, a centralized dictatorship, and said that haughtiness exists among its bishops, clergy, and believers. Osipov was forty-eight at the time of his renouncement. He was a professor at the Leningrad Seminary and was married a second time. According to Canon Law he could not serve as a priest, but was permitted to teach. After his renouncement, the Patriarch of Moscow unfrocked him but not before he was recruited as an anti-religious writer.[88] Anti-religious propagandists and agitators are officially recognized professionals in the Soviet Union.

One of the most popular, best known, and attractively prepared publications of anti-religious propaganda in the Soviet Union is *Nauka i zhisn*,[89] which began publication in 1958. It is richly illustrated with a colored cover, and its circulation is 150,000 to 195,000 copies a month. It is written for those with an above average education. Articles are directed toward teachers and professionals and appear in a special section—"*Nauka i religia.*"[90] Sample titles are: "The Myth about an After Life," "Animal Electricity," "Freedom of the Will," and "Teachers and Religion."

In this publication an attack on religion is made through the use of logic and the natural and social sciences. Reasoning seems to be central to each theme. Religion is pictured as a drag on progress, a method of enslavement of mankind, an interference with scientific progress, a darkener of men's minds, an unsocial way of life, an exploiter of people, an illogical ideology, an abuser of logic, and an enemy of Soviet life. Magazines and books which are of an anti-religious theme can be readily and very cheaply purchased.

As stated earlier, the tone in propaganda against religion changed in 1959. Articles using names of people and places began to appear. The Orthodox Church began to be an object of attack. In August, *Pravda*[91] attacked the clergy as being unlawful because they were carrying on activities not allowed them by the law such as calling places holy, displaying relics for veneration, and instructing children in religion. *Komsomol'skaia pravda* was more direct.[92] It made attacks on the main shrine of the Patriarchate, the Troitsk-Sergeiyevska Lavra at Zagorsk, as a hang-out for parasites where monks eat too much and

[87] Alexander Osipov, "A Rejection of Religion is the Only True Path," *Pravda*, December 6, 1959, p. 4.
[88] *Izvestia*, December 20, 1959, p. 6.
[89] *Science and Life.*
[90] *Science and Religion.*
[91] *Pravda*, August 21, 1959, "Concerning Scientific Propaganda."
[92] *Komsomol'skaia pravda*, August 13, 1959.

do nothing for mankind. Articles of the same kind were written concerning the Pskov Pechersk Monastery and the monks living there. Bishop Sergei of Astrakhan was then singled out for criticism. He was said to be living in great wealth and using his money to lead a licentious life and to pay criticizers blackmail. *Pravda*[93] had a similar article naming Father Terenty, Archbishop Anthony of Stavropol and Bakir, and accusing them of much the same errors. It was also stated that certain clergy beat their wives and were very cruel to them. These articles were written to undermine the image of the clergy. *Literaturnaia gazeta*[94] had much the same to say about monks, but a new line of thinking began to appear. Nuns were discussed and were accused of being collaborationists with the Germans during the war. A whole page was used to show their pictures and the captions said they looked pure and holy BUT . . .

Trud[95] had an article which summed up all the complaints. The lives of "about 250 students of the religious academy and seminary at Zagorsk (home of the Moscow institutions) " are explained. They are drinkers and lead immoral lives in town. The article bluntly states that if this goes on in the open, "behind the walls even more terrible things go on." The integrity and honesty of the monks who man the stalls where holy oil and water are sold are also disputed. They are accused of "pocketing the money." Names are given of men who have forsaken their families to become monks and to spend their time in drinking and carousing all night in their cells. On the other hand, the writer attacks the "brutal regime in the seminary and academy . . . resulting in seminarians going mad and committing suicide." The seminarians are bad also because they make raids on bookshops and newsstands and buy all the anti-religious literature and thus make it unavailable for the residents of the area. These raids "constitute a gross violation of the constitution" and should be stopped by the authorities.

Attacks and criticism on the Orthodox Church seem to be given such a prominent place in publications because "Orthodox ideology is trying to adapt itself to socialist reality."[96] Communist youth publications disparage the concept of peaceful coexistence between the Church and the State on the ground that it is misleading the youth into complacency concerning anti-religious activity.

Izvestia was even more explicit. It clearly states that the ideology of the Church "still remains incompatible with our communist ideology. The clergy even when they support the domestic and foreign

---

[93] *Pravda,* May 10, 1960.
[94] *Literaturnaia gazeta,* March 5, 1960.
[95] *Trud,* April 17, 1960.
[96] *Voprosy filosofii,* No. 3, 1961, pp. 3–7.

policies of the Soviet Socialist State remain as ever our ideological adversaries, and we are waging and shall continue to wage an ideological struggle with them."[97]

To wage this struggle, articles during this same period call upon the social scientist to make demographic and ethnographic studies of the problem areas to uproot religion from among the people. It was felt that the needs of the people during the war and the instabilities during that period turned those who were not fully atheistic to religion. Visitors coming in from capitalistic nations were also bringing adverse thoughts to the waverers. It was also felt that the figures given earlier for conversions to atheism were too high.

The number of anti-religious books released was increased. These books were written at various levels to appeal to many segments of the citizenry. Among the books printed in 1959 were 95,000 copies of *Ot Mraka k svetu*,[98] which is a collection of tales and excerpts from romantic novels concerning religion written by both Soviet and non-Soviet authors. The theme stressed is the reactionary role religion has taken in society in Russia and in Western Europe.

Excerpts of materials against religion taken from the works of great Russian writers like Pushkin, Chekov, and Tolstoy were reproduced in *Russkie pisateli o religii*,[99] of which 50,000 copies were printed.

Selections from the work of an outstanding atheistic author, Ivan Skvorchov-Stepanov (1870–1928), were published in a paperback edition of 100,000 copies, and it became part of the Popular Library of Atheism. *Blagochestivie rasmishleniia*[100] is a reflection upon hell and paradise, devils and angels, and the ways to salvation. It is written in popular easily read language. Skvorchov-Stepanov considered religion an exploitative element in society.

During the following year 10,000 copies of *O religii i tzerkvi*[101] were released. It consists of essays of Dobrolubov (1836–1861), who was one of the outstanding representatives of atheistic thought in Russia in the nineteenth century. The selections in this book emphasize the need for social reforms and the shortcomings of religion in general and of Russian Orthodoxy in particular.

In 1961 three thousand copies of *Russkoe narodnoe poeticheskoe tvorchestvo protiv tzerkvi i religii*[102] were released through the Academy of Sciences of the U.S.S.R. This book differs from the others in its content. It consists of parodies of Church prayers and the Sacred

[97] *Izvestia*, February 18, 1961.
[98] *From Darkness to Light.*
[99] *Russian Writers on Religion.*
[100] *Devout Reflections.*
[101] *Concerning Religion and the Church.*
[102]*Russian People's Poetical Creative Works Against the Church and Religion.*

Scriptures written in a style to obtain a comic effect or ridicule. For example, the Lord's Prayer is divided into eighteen phrases between which are interjected two or three sentences of narrative which gives a sacrilegious effect when read in its totality.[103] The metre of the church tones and the chants of the priest are also mimicked to obtain the same over-all effect of comedy and ridicule.

Proizhozhdeniia hristianskoho kul'ta[104] is another paperback. It examines some of the sacraments of the Church and the development of the Orthodox Church as a cult, indicating that religion is an exploitative element in society and has no place in modern Soviet society. This book specifically discusses spirituality and religious customs.

The most formidable reference book is *Sputnik ateista*.[105] A revised and enlarged edition presenting systematic arguments against religious concepts was published in 1961 in 180,000 copies. The research was under the guidance of academically trained people from the departments of history and philosophy. It examines the origins of religion and the fundamental religious movements of both East and West up to their present status in the U.S.S.R. Various sections of the book examine the Bible, the Koran, religious holidays and customs, give popular proverbs about religion and comments from atheists all over the world, and contain illustrations related to specific religions.

Other books on the same subject were printed during these years and, when the Twenty-second Congress of the Communist Party met on October 17, 1961, it stressed the need for more scientific-atheistic propaganda.

In reviewing the Soviet press of 1961, scant references could be found to a True Orthodox Church which appears to be a catacomb church and not under the jurisdiction of the Patriarchate.

From the examples cited, the impression is gleaned that at this time the drive against the Patriarchate has moved into a new and more intensive phase.

[103]*Ibid.*, pp. 26–27.
[104] *Origin of the Christian Cult.*
[105] *Sputnik of the Atheist.*

CHAPTER VII

Communist Philosophy Unchanged

The destruction of religion is assigned to the prior power, the Party. The leader in the Soviet Union is such by virtue of his position in the Party and not by virtue of the governmental office he may hold. N. S. Khrushchev, for example, did not become Chairman of the Council of Ministers until January, 1958, but his predominance was assured from late 1953 when he was named First Secretary of the Party, the highest position in the Party and therefore in the Soviet Union. Article 126 of the Soviet Constitution states, "the Party is the vanguard of the working people in their struggle to build communist society and it is the leading core of all organizations of the working people, both public and state."[1]

When the 1945 regulations concerning the Church were adopted by the Provincial Sobor, the pressures of a Nazi invasion made it essential to receive the support of all segments of Soviet society; therefore, J. V. Stalin made concessions to the Church. Since then the earlier methods of violence against the Church have been abandoned in favor of education and persuasion.

It is of importance to know that the law in the U.S.S.R. protects the right of the atheist and not the believers. The decree of April 8, 1929, which was promulgated by the All-Russian Central Executive Committee and the Council of People's Commissars gives ample illustrations of the limitations placed on religion in general and on the Church in particular.

This position is based upon the basic philosophy of the Communists. The central core of Communist philosophy is based upon a belief that religion is but a by-product of the basic factors of social life which

---

[1] Denisov and Kirichenko, *op. cit.*, p. 406.

are economic. Marx and Lenin believed that religion was the worst implement of class exploitation. This is relevant to the basic philosophy of Communism which makes one of its primary missions the dissolving of social classes. They believed this could be accomplished by destroying the worst implement of class exploitation—religion. They further tended to justify their action against a belief in God by their own belief in pure materialism. The conclusion which Communists draw from this makes up their code of conduct toward ideologies in general and religion in particular.

Adolph Keller, the former director of the Ecumenical Seminar in Geneva, and a consultant to the World Council of Churches, has summed up the open hostility of the Communists against the Church by stating that it is based on three roots:

> The first is the inherent materialism and declared atheism of the Marxian social philosophy. The second is the hatred of religion which under the Czarist regime was responsible for the tyranny, the capitalistic exploitation of the people, and caused the most violent subsequent reaction. The third root is the new belief in the omnipotence of science as opposed to religion.[2]

Upon coming into power the Party began within a few months to apply its ideology in the field of religion. The Communist ideology was originally derived from a view of history and this is still at the very core of Communism. Since history is primarily concerned with the field of human activities, Marx built a comprehensive theory around what he believed to be the motivational factors guiding the destiny of man. One can readily see from reading Marx that the guidance he offers is similar to that offered by religion, whose core is also belief, and thus can be used as a replacement by those who no longer believe in God as a rule to live by. He believed that property brought about a division of society into classes and that property was a powerful weapon of control in shaping the destiny of man; therefore, one of his main concerns was to eliminate private property. The basic elements of Marxian belief are to be found in the *Communist Manifesto* first published in 1848. The *Communist Manifesto* itself is a mixture of historical fact and myth. Through a bit of sociological analysis which is designed to arouse sympathy and indignation in the reader by stating that the laborer must sell himself and thus expose himself to indignities, Marx drives a strong current of emotionalism into this manifesto. This sociological analysis is used to justify a total rejection of the previous social order in which a belief in God was a very formative and central ideology. He believed that out of

[2] Keller, *op. cit.*, pp. 48–49.

this class struggle flowed many other problems that could only be solved by the Communist philosophy which held the key that would open the door of perpetual gratification for man. The *Communist Manifesto* advocated the redeeming cause of the proletariat and therefore affirms that any action in this direction is morally justifiable. By this insistence it comes into direct conflict with the central value system of religion, which is the freeing of man from sin and not from economic problems alone.

Because religion does not stand by itself but rather within an organized institution known as the Church, it has certain specific and inherent properties; consequently, once Communism came into power in Russia, Lenin began applying the theories of Marx directly against the institution. Communism is atheistic and thus against any belief in God. It is doubtful that Marx had the Russian Orthodox Church in mind; it is more probable that he was thinking of the Roman Catholicism and, or, Protestantism when he wrote. Since his theory was atheistic, it was able to be applied against any body of religious beliefs. The rejection of a belief in God is very essential to Communist thinking and is partially derived from Feuerbach's idea that God is man's own invention and that in reality there is nothing beyond nature-matter. In the *Selected Works of Lenin* published in London in 1939, Lenin says that the dictum of Marx, "Religion is the opium of the people," is the cornerstone of the whole Marxist view on religion. Lenin further states that Marx regarded all modern religions, churches, and religious organizations as instruments of bourgeois reaction which serve to defend class exploitation and to drug the working class. He further states that materialism is absolutely atheistic and resolutely hostile to religion.[3]

Lenin himself went considerably beyond Marx and Engels in his hostility to religion.

> Every religious idea, every idea of god, every flirtation with the idea of god, is unutterable vileness. . . . Any person who engages in building a god, or who even tolerates the idea of god-building, disparages himself in the worst possible fashion.[4]

It should be noted that Lenin had stated these opinions before coming to power. Lenin substituted class struggle for human virtue. Class struggle therefore is the basis for Lenin's formation of Communist morality.

From the readings of Lenin it becomes obvious that religious ethics

[3] Lenin, "The Attitude of the Workers' Party Toward Religion," May, 1909, Vol. XI in *Selected Works* (London: Lawrence and Wishart, Ltd., 1939), pp. 633–664.
[4] Lenin, "Letters from Lenin to A. M. Gorky," November 14, 1913, *ibid.*, pp. 675–676.

and morality are repudiated and that morality is entirely subordinated to the interests of class struggle and that one of the main struggles is against religion. Thus, after the rejection of God and the discarding of any notion of good that men as such have in common, open warfare was declared against the teaching of religion and the Church. This vacuum previously filled by a belief in God was replaced by a new value system which was intensely preoccupied with imbuing the people of Russia with Communist ethics and morality. Although theoretically Communism is based upon stressing the common good of the individual, freeing the working man from exploitation, rewarding each one according to his ability and needs, and teaching that the State would eventually wither away, thus making central authority unnecessary, these premises are not as yet realities in Soviet Russia. In practice, Communism in this sense does not exist in any Communist State today and there is no indication that it will be obtained in the foreseeable future. What in reality does exist is a totalitarian and monolithic structure which controls all human and material resources through a complicated governmental structure that is the most bureaucratic hierarchy in any present society. The Party's inner leadership has placed severe limitations upon religion, the Church, and the individual. Whatever consideration the Communist regime gives to the needs and desires of the individual is for the purpose of meeting the needs of the State. In examining the strategy and the tactics used by the Communists against religion and the Church in the Soviet Union, we find that force was its main implement in the early years, thus clearly demonstrating that the ends justify the means and that this dictum was strongly and regularly endorsed by the followers of Marx and Lenin.

Even though Stalin differed with Lenin, the differences were only a matter of degree. Stalin continued to advocate and emphasize the destruction of religion and the elimination of the Church in his actions. The large-scale actions of violence by Lenin and Stalin were provoked by what they believed in as Communists and were based upon privately instigated actions which were dictated by circumstances. Lenin's position is best and most completely detailed in the decrees stated on January 23/February 5, 1918. It is further illustrated by the action taken by the Eighth Congress of the Party of the Soviet Union held in March of 1919, which advocated absolute separation of religion from the schools and a most critical examination of the basis of religious belief. Again, at the Tenth Congress of the Party of the Soviet Union, which began on March 8, 1921, Lenin sanctioned widespread anti-religious agitation and propaganda among the masses.

At the Twelfth Congress in April, 1923, through Lenin's leadership, directives provided for special organizations to foster anti-religious progaganda, publish special literature, and establish anti-religious seminaries under competent Party leadership. For Lenin there was no room for toleration. To this date, Lenin, who died in January, 1924, remains the leading theoretician among the followers of Marx, and the most nimble, effective, and practical politician that Communism has ever had. Much discomfort and sorrow in this world could have been spared if the basic ideas of Lenin had been more widely known. He had very little confidence in man as an individual but had great confidence in organizations whose primary units were composed of highly selected professional revolutionaries under the control of a highly centralized power structure. He stressed that Communists had every right to be secretive and dishonest toward non-Communists, thus giving them a legal right to infiltrate other institutions and, wherever possible, to ruthlessly uproot opposing institutions and ideologies. These tactics were the basic guidelines of his successor, Stalin.

Since Lenin's death there have been no new additions or modifications of basic Marxist-Leninist thought. Stalin's administration, 1924 to March, 1953, was stronger in practical administration and organizational ability than in theorizing. Stalin adapted Lenin's policies to the needs of his time. The basic tensions between religion, Church, and Communist ideology continued. During Stalin's time the dictum "the ends justify the means" was particularly expressed by the dividing and conquering of his personal foes. He was less open and more deceitful in his dealings with the Church, and in general advocated less violent methods of suppression. Perhaps he understood religion and its implications more clearly than did Lenin, as he had spent several years in a Russian Orthodox Theological Seminary.[5] During the early years of his administration, he encouraged the split in the Russian Orthodox Church not because he favored any one side but rather because he knew that internal strife would weaken the Church. Stalin made several concessions to religion and the Church, most of which proved to be only maneuvers and strategems of expediency. Among the more important maneuvers was the acceptance of the declaration of loyalty by Metropolitan Sergius. This was a strategic move by Stalin because it alienated the sanctioning of hostile activities against the government by the Russian Orthodox hierarchy which was abroad, while at the same time it called upon the faithful within the Soviet Union to accept and openly support the Soviet regime.

The first Five Year Plan adopted in 1928 included an anti-religious

[5] Tiflis, Georgia.

program. In April, 1929, a decree laying down regulations concerning religion was enacted. The closing of churches continued and instruction in schools became anti-religious. The government continued to regard the Church with distrust and hostility. Anti-religious propaganda became an integral part of the Communist youth organizations and of the Militant Atheist Leagues. There was an abundance of anti-religious literature published during this period. The Constitution of 1936, surely guided by Stalin's values, struck out the Churches' freedom laid down in Article 13 of the 1918 Constitution: "Freedom of religious and anti-religious propaganda is conceded in behalf of all citizens;" instead it read, "Freedom for religious cults to function and freedom for anti-religious cults to function and freedom for anti-religious propaganda are conceded in behalf of all citizens."[6]

The churches continued to be closed and thus the theory of Lenin was continued in practice. The State supported anti-religious propaganda and the formation of atheistic units among the youth, the military, and the general public. It was not until three months after the outbreak of the war that the publication of the anti-religious journals was discontinued "because of the paper shortage." The anti-religious museums were also closed and the heavy taxes on the churches instituted by Stalin were substantially reduced. This was another maneuver based on circumstances and expediency dictated by the war conditions.

The Communists find no ethical counterdiction when, for example, they extend a friendly hand to religion one year and the next year persecute it; or when they ally themselves with democracy at one time, and the next time seek to overthrow it; or when they sign a treaty . . . and then fight against it.[7]

As has been previously indicated, what furthers the cause of the Party is morally correct to the Communists. Therefore, there is no limit to how often they may change their tactics.

As Lenin said: "It is necessary . . . to use any ruse, cunning, unlawful method, evasion, concealment of truth." Stalin added approvingly: "Dictatorship means nothing more nor less than the power which directly rests on violence which is not limited by any laws or restricted by any absolute rules."[8]

---

[6] Barron and Waddams, *op. cit.*, pp. 16–17.
[7] Lenin, "The Infantile Sickness of Leftism in Communism," quoted in Fulton J. Sheen, *Communism and the Conscience of the West* (New York: The Bobbs-Merrill Company, 1948), p. 66.
[8] Stalin, "Problems of Leninism," quoted in *ibid.*, p. 67.

When examining the Communist attitude toward religion, it is essential to remember that Communism is not only atheistic but militantly so and demands complete loyalty of its subjects and therefore is totalitarian. Of more recent origin, Communism is antagonistic to religion because it claims to be a scientific world-view and, in the minds of the Communists, religion presents the unscientific which to Lenin, in particular, meant it was reactionary.

Some of Stalin's expressions of expediency were the giving of decorations to clergy during World War II and permitting the Patriarchate to open seminaries, to publish a religious journal, and to hold a national Church Sobor. At the same time, he set up a liaison with the rank of full minister and retained the Forty-eight Paragraphs as conditions of control which were accepted by the hierarchy at the national Provincial Sobor in 1945. A legally registered group is easier to observe than an unorganized movement. There is no doubt that the Nazi invasion and the need of the fullest cooperation and assistance from the Allies were at stake. Pressing circumstances prompted these tactical maneuvers.

After Stalin's death, Nikita Khrushchev, who was then First Secretary of the Communist Party of the Soviet Union, continued to uphold the Communist philosophy and to perpetuate the Communist position. On November 10, 1954, he criticized the shortcomings and errors of the scientific-atheistic propaganda that was being disseminated among the populace of the Soviet Union.[9] On January 9, 1960, the Central Committee under his leadership issued a statement in an article entitled: "Concerning the Problem of Party Propaganda in Contemporary Conditions" in which there is criticism of the passivity of pushing forth Marxist-Leninist ideology and the calling of women to be particularly active in their political life "to fight against religious prejudice and also the survival of the petty bourgeoisie."[10] In anti-religious journals we find the same philosophical tone.

Freedom of conscience for parents who are believers must not be turned into a denial of the freedom of the public and the state to intervene positively in questions of family training. . . . It is necessary to raise the question of the lawful defense of the persons of children from religious intoxication and violence . . . our public and our legal organs must enter into the defense of children subjected to spiritual and moral mutilation on the part of the parents; they must enter into the freedom of conscience of the rising generation. . . . The truly revolutionary humanism of

[9] *Sputnik ateista,* 2d ed., (Moscow: Gospolitizdat, 1961), pp. 458–462.
[10] *Ibid.,* p. 462.

Soviet legislation and the lofty principles of Communist morality demand this.[11]

In 1961 the "Situation of the Administration of the Church" was amended, disrupting the hierarchal chain of command by placing more authority in the local civil (Communist) leaders, and thus returning to the spirit of the laws of 1929 when stricter control of the Church by the State existed.

It is clear from the foregoing that the Party and the State continue to be not only anti-religious but absolutely dogmatic regarding the conscience of its people and especially those under eighteen. The basic Communist philosophy as stated by Marx and Lenin stands unchanged.

[11] E. Filimonov, *Molodoi kommunist*, No. 10, October, 1959, quoted in Paul Geren, "Soviet Union and U.S.," *Church and State*, Vol. III (May, 1961), pp. 66–67.

CHAPTER VIII

New Era of Adjustments

On July 18, 1961, in the Troitsk-Sergeivska Lavra (Monastery at Zagorsk), the central meeting place for conferences of bishops and the location of a theological institution, a council of hierarchs met for the purpose of updating the Forty-eight Paragraphs.

This Sobor presided over by Patriarch Alexei was the first meeting of all the hierarchs concerning the treatise on the "Situation of the Administration of the Church" since 1945. The Patriarch explained that social changes were occurring at a very rapid pace and consequently demanded a discussion and a re-evaluation of some of the points of the treatise and that he anticipated the need for more meetings called at shorter intervals. He considered one of the main concerns to be to bring about order on the parish level because in many places of the various dioceses, disturbances had occurred which resulted in unending complaints and disorders. He said:

> You can't imagine the flood of complaints from places to the Patriarchate and to the Soviets on matters concerning the Russian Orthodox Church and even to our higher governmental institution—the Soviet of Ministers of the U.S.S.R.—that have been received. Complaints about disorders in parishes, complaints of clerics against the parochial administrators, and the administrators upon the rectors and parish clerics, and complaints against the Patriarchate and the Holy Synod who in their opinion are doing nothing about the registered complaints.[1]

The Patriarch continued:

> A year ago the Holy Synod brought to the attention of the Diocesan hierarchs the fact that Soviet laws concerning religion had been broken and gave directives to alleviate this situation;

[1] *Zhurnal*, No. 8, 1961, p. 5.

nevertheless, complaints continued to be received. It was then decided that simple palliative measures were not enough and that decisive means had to be promulgated which would result in strict regulations which would bind the clerics and the parishes' administrative organs.[2]

In April, 1961, the "Soviet on Matters Concerning the Russian Orthodox Church" informed the Synod that the Soviet of Ministers of the U.S.S.R. brought their attention to the many infractions of the Soviet laws by the clergy and demanded the restoration of order in the life of the parish, particularly in matters of the financial-economic aspect in accordance with the laws regulating the cult.

The first change in the Forty-eight Paragraphs[3] was made by the Holy Synod on April 18, 1961. It was decreed that the rector would be freed from participating in the financial-economic matters of the parish and he would be concerned only with the Divine Services and spiritual matters. It was pointed out that this was in agreement with the book of Acts 6:2–3. At this conference it was further stated that this decision should not disturb the rector because it would give him more time for spiritual guidance.

Second, this Sobor of hierarchs decided that it was expedient to increase the number of permanent members of the Holy Synod because the three permanent members were located at a great distance from Moscow. The two permanent members added to the Holy Synod hold the rank of bishop—Head of the External Affairs Department, and the Administrator of the Moscow Diocese. This decision was made on March 16, in session with the Holy Synod and the Patriarch, and confirmed at this Council of Hierarchs. This was an addition to the Part II, Numbers 18 and 19, of the Forty-eight Paragraphs, which calls for three permanent members of the Holy Synod and three temporary members.[4] The original three permanent members were the Metropolitans of Kiev, Leningrad, and Krutitsk. The two new permanent members added are both of the younger generation and have lived most of their lives under the Soviet regime. The chronology (1961) indicates that one of these is Archbishop Nikodim, thirty-two years old, who appears to be helping Patriarch Alexei, eighty-four years of age, administer the Patriarchate. Officially, Archbishop Nikodim is in charge of the External Affairs Department of the Patriarchate, the international department whose sphere is expanding.

Third, Paragraph 30 omitted the last sentence concerning the

[2] *Ibid.*, p. 6.
[3] See Appendix F.
[4] *Zhurnal*, No. 8, 1961, p. 9.

specific obligation and responsibility of deans. It took away their authorization to oversee matters regarding the economic life of the parish.

The primary concern of the Sobor of hierarchs was to change the provisions in Part IV concerning parishes, Paragraphs 35 to 48.[5] This was brought about by the higher ranking archbishops who spoke about the necessity of bringing about an accommodation by the Church to the government demands. All of the speeches by the hierarchs were in favor of Part IV being changed to eliminate the conflict which had arisen, first of all, between clerics and laymen, and to stress their absolute belief that the changes would be for the benefit of the Church.

The blame for the conflict was unequivocally and absolutely laid at the doorstep of the clerics.[6] No criticism of laymen was registered. Furthermore, the hierarchs stated that during the interim April 18 to July 18, 1961, everyone in their dioceses who spoke on the matter was pleased with the changes that were recommended in this Part IV and that even the clergy of the Moscow diocese accepted them with enthusiasm.

The proposed changes were accepted unanimously and were to be published in the *Zhurnal,* stating that the means taken should benefit parish life and that they were in conjunction and in agreement with the governmental laws of 1929 concerning religious groups in the U.S.S.R. It was further stressed that the changes enacted would remain in effect until the next Provincial Sobor of the Russian Orthodox Church. No date was set for this nor was a promise to set the date made. The Patriarchate's power was cut back and the clergy were hemmed in by the Soviet government—a harbinger was released.

---

[5] See Appendix F.
[6] *Zhurnal,* No. 8, 1961, p. 6.

CHAPTER IX

Conclusion

In Czarist Russia the Russian Orthodox Church gained a privileged position which became prestigious. In the area of religion it held exclusive status over all other confessions. With the favors thus accorded the Orthodox Church came the price which religion pays for State favors—State interference in religious affairs. The czars and their successors, especially from the time of Peter the Great, called and dismissed members of the hierarchy. They also enforced unity of belief and practice upon the citizens. Although each czar bore his own influence upon the Church, it did not result in any dramatic changes in the essential relationship previously established; at best it was only a variation in tactics. The Church paid for the privileged status conferred upon it by the State, for the laws that protected it also regulated it.

The first encounter of the Church with an atheistic ruler was ushered in by the Revolution of 1917, with the subsequent seizure of power by the Communists, who set in motion a program which looked toward the ultimate elimination of all religious influence in the U.S.S.R. The Communist Party which controls the Soviet State is not only totalitarian but avowedly atheistic. Its intensive drive to eliminate all private opinions and convictions and to bring its citizens into complete submission and surrender became especially obvious in the area of religion. A period of outright persecution began in 1918 and continued through 1938. This began by confiscating all of the properties of the Church and by harassing the central administration of the Church, the clergy, and the believers. Many thousands of churches were closed. The clergy were disenfranchised. In reality the Orthodox Church became an illicit social organization; the Patriarch and thousands of its members were declared guilty of conspiracy to commit treason. The alignment of some believers with the pro-czarist elements which fought in the Civil War enraged the Communists.

Along with this anti-religious policy an intensive campaign was inaugurated to organize the youth into cells for the study of scientific enlightenment to combat religious influences. This group helped influence legislation in 1929 and 1932 which brought the Church into submission and supervised activities.

The toleration of the State is a belated acknowledgment of religion; however, the State has no room for a toleration of religious propaganda. The rulers of the U.S.S.R. have imposed upon the Church a frame of reference for perceiving, thinking, and acting which is related to the Communist's belief that no God exists and that religion is an invention of man for exploiting the uneducated, gullible, and superstitious. They believe it must be combatted and destroyed and completely eliminated from the Soviet scene.

Because the Communist Party rules the U.S.S.R., it is in a powerful and exalted position. Its influence is vast. Its strength is tremendous. The Church has no channels of free communication or expression. No overt expression of public opinion exists in the U.S.S.R. and for this reason the *Zhurnal,* the official paper of the Church, reflects the policy of the State and never states an attitude or opinion which is contrary to the position of the State. The State acts with impunity toward the Church, and the Church has no alternative but to respond with forbearance toward the State. In nearly half a century of Communist control, the State has penetrated into almost every aspect of Church life.

In contrast to the Czarist era, the State makes no direct grant of public funds to the Orthodox Church. The laws of 1918 expressed prohibitions against State subsidies to the Church and confiscated its holdings. These laws state that the State is not only separated from the Church but it is restricted from helping the Church and is putting serious limitations upon it. The provisions preclude State appropriations for any of the programs of the Church. It is prohibited from creating and maintaining any type of welfare or assistance programs for believers or non-believers. These rulings are upheld and strengthened by the laws of 1929 and 1932. The Church cannot hold any valuables or properties without the permission of civil authorities. It cannot bind its members to any financial obligations. It can only use state property provided the State has no other designation for the building and the building meets standards required by the civil engineers and civil authorities. The Church has no priority for building materials for building or for repairs even if repairs are deemed necessary by the authorities.

In the social area, the Church cannot mobilize public opinion in support of religious liberty, nor can it resist the State's advances to suppress it. It cannot invoke the aid of the courts in maintaining the integrity of the Constitution with respect to the separation of the Church and the State. It has no right of a legal entity. It is a Church that has been muted except when the State finds it advisable to do otherwise.

In addition to the laws of 1918, 1929, and 1932, other controls have been set up to assure the smooth functioning of relations between the two institutions. After 1938 when war clouds were gathering in Europe, the State became preoccupied with international matters. Soon after the Nazis invaded, regulations controlling the Church-State situation were ratified by the leaders of the Church, and a department was set up by the State headed by a full ranking minister to inaugurate coordination. The Forty-eight Paragraphs of 1945 adopted by the Church at a Sobor define the limits of authority and responsibility of every adherent of the Orthodox faith from the Patriarch to the unordained believer. At this point the Church was actually faced with two alternatives, either to wither away and cease existing altogether or to retain just enough inner freedom to be able to be called a Church. The Church leaders selected the latter course.

The Forty-eight Paragraphs regulating the interaction gave no freedom of religion beyond the opportunity to attend a limited number of government-licensed churches. To the Communists, Orthodoxy was simply and exclusively a cult, a system of worshipping a deity with a certain rite which was accorded to be a superstition. The Orthodox believer was not encouraged to pursue his religion as a way of life because it was separate and contrary to the value system of the Communists. The civil authorities did not interfere with the structure of divine services, nor were the musical compositions changed or modified; nevertheless, the government did affect the circumstances of those who were active in the church choirs and in the performance of these divine services. Gradually, the Church lost most of its trained personnel because of pressures put upon them. The remaining personnel were compelled to participate in an uneven struggle because if they wished to continue in their work they had to obtain the endorsement of the government. This is referred to in paragraphs 16 and 48 as "has his own seal and stamp registered with the appropriate government authority."

The regulations of 1945 were much more liberal toward the Church leaders than the modifications set forth in the amendments of 1961. The congregation was granted independent standing and is now answerable to the government directly in the economic and financial areas. These amendments contradict the canons of the Church because authority is taken away from the ecclesiastical leaders where it was traditionally and canonically held. The laws governing the Church have been progressively more coercive from 1918 to 1961.

Because the letter of the law must be adhered to and is enforced in the U.S.S.R., the Church has been narrowed within the country, but outside the U.S.S.R. it has been widening its sphere of influence. It appears that conditions under which the Church will operate in the future within the U.S.S.R. will be even more limiting. Internationally, the sphere will continue to widen. At home churches and seminaries are being closed, while abroad representatives of the Church are participating in world-wide ecumenical and peace conferences.

The education of the clergy is restricted to the training of ritualistic technicians. The curriculum apparently does not prepare the graduate to come to grips with contemporary society. The more recent changes indicate that the training has become narrower and shallower. It has relegated intellectual learning to a much lower rung than ritual and belief. In this area, the Communist system has made a significant impact. Between 1944 and 1947 eight seminaries and two academies were opened; however, it appears that by 1962 only three seminaries and two academies were still open. If the number of churches are open which are claimed to be open, most of them would have pastors who are not graduates of a theological seminary. The clergy's destiny is related to how well they fit into the complex bureaucracy of the monolithic system.

Very little has been printed in the U.S.S.R. which could be classified as religious publications. The few books that have been printed are directly related to the liturgical services or to the conditions under which the Church operates. The only regular publication is the *Zhurnal Moskovskoi Patriarchii,* which seems to be limited to eighty pages an issue. It gives every indication that a free press does not exist for the Church. The anti-religious press (atheistic) and general Soviet press have full and exclusive rights of mass media. The *Zhurnal* never reflects any attacks made upon the Church. Since 1959 the anti-religious press has increased and intensified its assaults on religion in general and has openly attacked the Orthodox Church which theretofore was seldom attacked. The number of anti-religious books released has been increased, as has been the stress on anti-religious education in the schools.

The destruction of religion is still in the core of Communist philosophy; however, the tactical approaches have varied from the crude to the more sophisticated. All segments of society are recruited in this confrontation.

The effects of the 1959 changes are evident in the 1961 amendments to the Forty-eight Paragraphs which guide the interaction between Church and State. It is believed that the Patriarchate's prerogatives are more limited and that an intensive drive against religion is in progress which may be more difficult to detect.

The sum total of the interaction since 1917 indicates that the future of the Orthodox Church depends upon its participation in the objectives of the government and upon the courage of the people to express their need for religion.

APPENDICES

APPENDIX A

Laws of 1918

Separation of the Church from the Government and the Schools from the Church[1]

Decree of the Soviet of People's Commissars
January 23, 1918[2]

1. The church is separated from the state.
2. Within the territory of the Republic, it is forbidden to pass any local laws or regulations which would restrain or limit the freedom of conscience or which would grant special rights or privileges on the basis of the religious confession of citizens.
3. Every citizen may confess any religion or profess none at all. Every legal restriction connected with the profession of certain faiths or with the profession of no faith is now revoked.
   Note: In all official documents every mention of a citizen's religious affiliation or nonaffiliation shall be removed.
4. The actions of the government or other organizations of public law may not be accompanied by any religious rights or ceremonies.
5. The free performance of religious rites is granted as long as it does not disturb public order or infringe upon the rights of citizens of the Soviet Republic. In such cases, the local authorities are entitled to take the necessary measures to secure public order and safety.
6. No one may refuse to carry out his citizen's duties on the grounds of his religious views.
   Exceptions to this provision may be permitted by special decisions to the people's court if one civil duty is substituted for another.
7. Religious vows or oaths are abolished.
   In necessary situations, a ceremonial promise will suffice.
8. The acts of a civil status are registered exclusively by the civil authorities: the departments for the registration of marriages and births.
9. The school is separated from the church.
   The teaching of religious doctrines in all state and public schools, or in private educational institutions where general subjects are taught, is prohibited. Citizens may receive and give religious instructions privately.
10. All ecclesiastical and religious associations are subject to the same general regulations pertaining to private associations and unions, and shall not enjoy

[1] *Kommunisticheskaia partiia i sovetskoe pravitel'stvo o religii i tzerkvi* (Moscow: Gospolitizdat, 1959), pp. 42–43.
[2] February 5, 1918, according to the Gregorian calendar.

117

any special privileges or subsidies either from the state or from local autonomous or self-governing institutions.

11. The compulsory exaction of collections or dues for the benefit of the ecclesiastical and religious association is prohibited, as well as any kind of coercion or infliction of punishment by these associations upon their members.

12. No ecclesiastical and religious association has the right to own property. They do not have the rights of a legal entity.

13. All property in Russia now owned by ecclesiastical and religious organizations is declared national property.

Buildings and objects intended especially for religious rites shall be handed over, by special decision of the local or central governmental authorities, free of charge for use to responsible religious associations.

President of the Soviet of People's Commissars
   V. Ul'anov (Lenin).

National Commissars:
   N. Podvoiski, V. Algasov,
   V. Trutovski, A. Shlichter,
   P. Prosh'an, V. Menzhinski,
   A. Shliapnikov, G. Petrovski.

Executive Officer:
   Vl. Bonch-Bruevich.

Secretary:
   N. Gorbunov.

Published according to "Collection of Indications and Decisions of the Workers—Peasants Government," No. 18, January 26, 1918.

Criminal Code Regarding Religion—1922

Infringement of the Regulations
for the Separation of Church and State

The Criminal Code has been in operation in the U.S.S.R. since June 1, 1922. It contains a special section dealing with "Infringement of the Regulations for the Separation of Church and State" (Section III, Articles 119–125, and Article 227).

SECTION III—*Infringement of the Regulations for the Separation of Church and State*[1]

ARTICLE 119—Whosoever utilizes the religious superstitions of the masses in order to plot against the Government of Workmen and Peasants or to instigate resistance to the laws and decrees of the said Government is liable to the penalty laid down in Article 69 of the Criminal Code. (This penalty is strict solitary confinement for a minimum term of three years.)

The same crime if committed in time of war or of popular uprisings is to be punished by the maximum penalty allowed by law.

Any incitement of the people to active or passive resistance to the orders of the central or local authorities, provided counter-revolutionary purposes have not been provided, is to be punished by the penalty laid down in Article 83 of the Criminal Code. (This penalty is strict solitary confinement for a maximum term of one year.)

If agitation or propaganda is carried on in time of war with the object of preventing citizens from fulfilling their military obligations, or obligations and duties in connection with military operatons, the penalty may be raised to the maximum.

ARTICLE 120—Whosoever uses fraudulent devices to excite the superstitious spirit of the masses or to obtain profit for himself is liable to imprisonment or hard labor for a maximum term of one year.

ARTICLE 121—The teaching of religious doctrine to persons under age in public and in private schools is to be punished by hard labour for a maximum term of one year.

[1] Francis McCullagh, *The Bolshevik Persecution of Christianity* (London: Billings and Sons, Ltd., 1924), pp. 357–358.

ARTICLE 122—Any pressure exercised in the collection of funds for ecclesiastical or religious organizations is to be punished by hard labour for a maximum term of six months, and two years' deprivation of the right of signing agreements with the local Soviets for the utilization of the property of the said organizations.

ARTICLE 123—Every religious or ecclesiastical body which usurps administrative or judicial rights to function, or assumes a public and official character, is to be punished by dissolution together with confiscation of its property, and its members are liable to hard labour for a maximum term of six months.

ARTICLE 124—The celebration of religious rites on the premises of State institutions and houses of business, and likewise the introduction of religious images into the said premises is to be punished by hard labour for a maximum term of three months, or a maximum fine of 300 gold roubles.

ARTICLE 125—Any hindrance offered to the performance of religious rites, in so far as the said rites do not offend against public order and are not accompanied by attacks on the rights of citizens, is to be punished by hard labour for a maximum term of six months.

*   *   *

ARTICLE 227—Any celebration of religious rites or ceremonies in violation of the rules and by-laws of local authorities for the regulation of traffic is punishable by hard labour or a maximum fine of 300 gold roubles.

APPENDIX C

Laws of 1929 and 1932

Law on Religious Associations, 1929

Laws on Religious Associations (O religioznykh ob'edineniakh) of April 8, 1929 as amended in 1932 changing only the names of the authorities.[1]

1. Churches, religious groups, sects, religious movements, and other associations for any cult or any denomination come under the Decree of January 23, 1918, on the Separation of the Church from the State and the School from the Church (Collection of Laws No. 18, 1918, text No. 203).
2. Religious associations of believers of all denominations shall be registered as religious societies or groups of believers.
   A citizen may be a member of only one religious association (society or group).
3. A religious society is a local association of not less than 20 believers who are 18 years of age or over and belong to the same cult, faith or sect, united for the common satisfaction of their religious needs. Believers who are not numerous enough to organize a religious society may form a group of believers. Religious societies and groups do not enjoy the rights of legal entity.
4. A religious society or group of believers may start its activities only after the registration of the society or group by the committee on religious matters at the proper city or district (raion) soviet.
5. In order to register a religious society at least 20 initiators must submit to the agencies mentioned in the previous Article an application in accordance with the form determined by the Permanent Committee for Religious Matters at the [Council of Ministers].
6. In order to register a group of believers, the representative of the group (Art. 13) must submit an application to the agencies mentioned in Article 4 of the city or district where the group is located in accordance with the form determined by the Permanent Committee for Religious Matters at the [Council of Ministers].
7. The registration agencies shall register the society or group within one month, or inform the initiators of the denial of the registration.
8. The registration agencies shall be informed on the composition of the society, as well as on their executive and accounting bodies and on the clergy, within the period and in accordance with the forms determined by the Permanent Committee for Religious Matters at the [Council of Ministers].

[1] Published in *Sobranie uzakonenii i rasporiazhenii rabochekrest'ianskogo pravitel'stva R.S.F.S.R.* (Collection of the Government of Workers and Peasants of the R.S.F.S.R.), No. 35, 1929, text No. 353, amendments *Sobranie uzakonenii,* No. 8, 1932, text No. 41, II, 6.

9. In the list of members of religious societies or groups of believers only believers who expressed consent thereto may be included.
10. For the satisfaction of their religious needs, the believers who have formed a religious society may receive from the district or city soviet, under a contract, free of charge, special prayer buildings and objects intended exclusively for the cult.

   Besides that the believers who have formed a religious society or group of believers may use for prayer meetings other premises left to them by private persons or local soviets on lease. Such premises shall be subject to all regulations provided for in the present Law relating to prayer buildings; the contracts for the use of such premises shall be concluded by individual believers on their personal responsibility. Such premises shall be subject to technical and sanitary regulations.

   A religious society or group of believers may use only one prayer building or [complex of] premises.
11. Transactions for the management and use of religious property, such as the hiring of watchmen, buying of fuel, repairing of the building and objects destined for the rite, purchasing of products or property necessary for a religious rite or ceremony, and other transactions closely and directly connected with the doctrine and ritual of the cult, as well as for the renting of premises, for prayer meetings, may be made by individual citizens who are members of the executive body of religious societies or are representatives of groups of believers.

   No contract embodying such arrangements may contain in its text any references to commercial or industrial transaction, even if these acts are of a kind directly connected with the affairs of the cult, such as the renting of a candle factory or a printing establishment for the printing of religious books, etc.
12. For each general assembly of a religious society or group of believers, permission shall be obtained: in cities from committees for religious matters of the city soviets, and in rural areas from the executive committees of the district.
13. For the accomplishment of functions connected with the management and use of the religious property (Art. 11), and for outside representation, the religious associations elect at their general assemblies executive bodies from among their members by open ballot—a religious society, an executive body of three members, and a group of believers with one representative.
14. The registration agencies are entitled to remove individual members from the executive body of a religious society or the representative elected by a group of believers.
15. The general assembly may elect an auditing committee of no more than three members for the examination of religious property and money collected by religious associations from their members as donations or voluntary offerings.
16. No permission of the government authorities is necessary for the meetings of the executive and auditing organs.
17. Religious associations may not: (a) Create mutual credit societies, cooperative or commercial undertakings, or in general, use property at their disposal for other than religious purposes; (b) give material help to their members; (c) organize for children, young people, and women special prayer or other meetings, circles, groups, departments for Biblical or literary study, sewing, working or the teaching of religion, etc., excursions, children's playgrounds, libraries, reading rooms, sanatoria, or medical care.

   Only books necessary for the purpose of the cult may be kept in the prayer buildings and premises.
18. Teaching of any kind of the religious cult in schools, boarding schools, or preschool establishments maintained by the State, public institutions or private persons is prohibited. Such teaching may be given exclusively in religious courses created by the citizens of the U.S.S.R. with the special per-

mission of the Permanent Committee for Religious Matters at the [Council of Ministers].

19. The activities of the clergymen, preachers, preceptors and the like shall be restricted to the area in which the members of their religious association reside and in the area where the prayer building or premises are situated.

The activities of clergymen, preachers and preceptors who permanently serve two or more religious associations shall be restricted to the area of residence of the believers who are members of such religious associations.

20. The religious societies and groups of believers may organize local, All-Russian or All-Union religious conventions or conferences by special permission issued separately for each case by:

(a) the Permanent Committee for Religious Matters of the [Council of Ministers] if an All-Russian or All-Union convention or congress on the territory of the RSFSR is supposed to be convoked.

(b) the local Committee for Religious Matters, if a local convention is supposed to be convoked.

The permission for convocation of republican conventions and conferences shall be granted by the Committee for Religious Matters of the appropriate republic.

21. Local, All-Russian and All-Union religious conventions and conferences may elect from among their members executive bodies in implementation of the decisions of the convention or conference. The list of members of the elected executive bodies shall be submitted simultaneously with the materials of the convention or conference to the authority which granted the permission for organizing the convention or conference in two copies in accordance with the form determined by the Permanent Committee for Religious Matters at the [Council of Ministers].

22. Religious congresses [and conventions] and executive bodies elected by them do not possess the rights of a legal entity and, in addition, may not:

(a) form any kind of central fund for the collection of voluntary gifts from believers;

(b) make any kind of obligatory collection;

(c) own religious property, receive the same by contract, obtain the same by purchase, or hire premises for religious meetings;

(d) conclude any kind of contracts or legal transactions.

23. The executive bodies of religious societies or groups, as well as religious conferences [and conventions], may use exclusively in religious matters stamps, seals and stationery with the imprint of their names. Such stamps, seals and stationery may not include emblems or slogans established for Soviet agencies.

24. Religious conventions and conferences may be initiated and convoked by religious societies and groups of believers, their executive bodies and executive bodies of religious conferences [or conventions].

25. Objects necessary for the rites of the cult, whether handed over under contract to the believers forming the religious association, acquired by them, or donated to them for the purpose of the cult, are nationalized and shall be under the control of the Committee for Religious Matters at the city or district soviet.

26. Premises used for the dwelling of a watchman which are located near the prayer building shall be leased together with other religious property to believers by contract, free of charge.

27. Prayer buildings and religious objects shall be leased to believers forming religious associations for use by the Committee for Religious Matters at the city or district soviet.

28. Prayer buildings with objects in these buildings shall be received by contract from the representatives of the district or city soviet by no less than 20 members of a religious society for use by all believers.

29. In the contract concluded between believers and the city or district soviet [it] shall be required that the persons who receive a prayer building and religious objects for use (Art. 28) shall:

(a) keep and take care of it as state property entrusted to them;
(b) repair the prayer building, as well as pay expenses connected with the possession and use of the building, such as heating, insurance, guarding, taxes [state, and] local, etc;
(c) use the property exclusively for the satisfaction of religious needs;
(d) compensate for any damage caused to the State by deterioration or defects of the property;
(e) keep an inventory of all religious objects in which [inventory] shall be entered all newly obtained objects for the religious cult either by purchase, donation, transfer from other prayer buildings, etc. which are not owned by individual citizens. Objects which become unfit for use shall be excluded from the inventory with the consent of the authority which concluded the contract;
(f) admit, without any hindrance, the representatives of the city or district soviet to exercise control over the property with the exception of the time when religious ceremonies are performed.

30. Prayer buildings of historical or artistic value registered as such in the Ministry of Education may be leased to believers on the same conditions, however, with the obligation to observe the regulations prescribed for registration and maintenance and the guarding of monuments of art and antiquity.

31. All local inhabitants of a corresponding faith have the right to sign the contract on the receipt of the buildings and religious objects for use and to obtain by this, after the leasing of property, similar rights of management over the property with persons who signed the original document.

32. Whoever has signed a contract may cancel his signature on the above-mentioned contract by filing the corresponding application to the agencies, enumerated in Article 4; this, however, does not free him from the responsibility for the good condition and safekeeping of the property during the period of the time prior to the filing of the above-mentioned application.

33. Prayer buildings shall be subject to compulsory fire insurance for the benefit of the appropriate local government at the expense of the persons who signed the contract. In case of fire, the insurance payment may be used for the reconstruction of the prayer building destroyed by fire, or upon decision of the appropriate local government for social and cultural needs of a given locality in full accordance with the Decree of August 24, 1925 on the Utilization of Insurance Payments Acquired for Prayer Buildings Destroyed by Fire.[2]

34. If there are no persons who wish to use a prayer building for the satisfaction of religious needs under the conditions provided for in Articles 27–33, the city or district soviet puts up a notice of this fact on the doors of the prayer building.

35. If, after the lapse of a week from the date of notice, no applications are submitted, the city or district soviet informs the higher authority. This information supplies data giving the date of the construction of the building and its condition, and the purpose for which the building is supposed to be used. The higher authority decides the further destination of the building in accordance with the provisions of Articles 40–42.

36. The transfer of a prayer building leased for the use of believers for other purposes (liquidation of the prayer building) may take place only according to a decision of the [Council of Ministers] of the autonomous republic or oblast which must be supported by reasons, in a case where the building is needed

[2] This law published in the Collection of R.S.F.S.R. Laws (*Sobranie uzakonenii Pravitel'stva R.S.F.S.R.*), No. 58, 1925, text 470, provides that, as a rule, the insurance payments shall be used for the reconstruction of the prayer building destroyed by fire (Arts. 1 and 2). However, they may be used also for cultural needs, if the local government has made a decision on the liquidation of the prayer building in this district (Art. 3). Such decision may be appealed before higher authorities and carried out only if the higher authority has confirmed the decision of the local government. If confirmed, the money may be used for cultural needs of the district in the location of the prayer building destroyed by fire.

for government or public purposes. The believers who formed the religious society shall be informed regarding such decision.

37. If the believers who formed the religious society appeal to the [Council of Ministers] within two weeks from the date of the announcement of the decision, the case on the liquidation of the prayer building shall be conveyed to the Council. If the [Council] confirms the decision, the contract with the believers becomes null and void, and the property shall be taken away from them.

38. The lease of nationalized or private houses for the needs of religious associations (Art. 10, par. 2) may be broken by a court decision in accordance with the general provisions of court procedure.

39. The liquidation of prayer buildings may be carried out in some instances by the Committee for Religious Matters by order of the city or district soviet in the presence of representatives of the local finance department and other interested departments as well as the representative of the religious association.

40. The religious property of the liquidated prayer buildings shall be distributed as follows:

    (a) all objects of platinum, gold, silver and brocade as well as jewels shall be included in the account of the State fund and transmitted for disposal by local financial agencies or the Ministry of Education, if the objects were registered there;

    (b) all objects of historical, artistic or museum value shall be transferred to the Ministry of Education;

    (c) other objects, such as sacred images, priestly vestments, banners, veils and the like, which have special significance for the performance of religious rites shall be entrusted to believers for use in other prayer buildings or premises; they shall be included in the inventory of religious property in accordance with the general rules;

    (d) such everyday objects as bells, furniture, carpets, chandeliers and the like shall be included in the account of the State fund and transmitted for disposal by local financial agencies of education if the objects were registered with these agencies;

    (e) so-called expendable property, such as money, frankincense, candles, oil, wine, wax, wood and coal, shall not be taken away if the religious association will continue to exist after the liquidation of the prayer building.

41. Prayer buildings and wayside shrines subject to liquidation, which are registered in special local agencies for State funds, may be transferred for use free of charge to proper executive committees or city soviets under the condition that they will be continuously considered as nationalized property and their use for other purposes than stipulated may not take place without the consent of the Minister of Finance.

42. Special local agencies for State funds shall register only such liquidated prayer buildings as are not included in the register of the Ministry of Education, such as monuments of art, or [those which] may not be used by local soviets as cultural or educational establishments (schools, clubs, reading halls, etc.) or dwelling houses.

43. When the religious association does not observe the terms of the contract or orders of the Committee for Religious Matters (on re-registration, repair, etc.), the contract may be annulled.

    The contract may also be annulled upon the presentation of lower executive committees by the [Council of Ministers] of the autonomous republic, oblast, etc.

44. When the decision of the authorities mentioned in Article 43 is appealed to the [Council of Ministers] within two weeks, the prayer building and property may actually be taken from the believers only after the final decision of [the Council].

45. The construction of new prayer buildings may take place upon request of religious societies under the observance of the general regulations pertaining to construction and technical rules as well as the special conditions stipulated

by the Permanent Committee for Religious Matters at the [Council of Ministers].

46. If the prayer building, because of dilapidation, threatens to fall apart completely or partly, the Committee for Religious Matters or the city or district soviet may request the executive body of the religious society or the representative of the group of believers to discontinue temporarily the holding of divine services and meetings of believers in such building until examined by the technical committee.

47. Simultaneously with the requirement on the closing of the prayer building, the officials exacting such requirement shall ask the appropriate agency of construction control to make a technical examination of the building. A copy of the letter shall be given to the agency which concluded the contract upon the leasing of the building and property to believers.

If the building is registered by the Ministry of Education, a copy shall be given to the appropriate agency of the Ministry.

48. The [following persons] shall be invited with the right of deliberative vote to the examination procedure by the technical committee:
   (a) the local representative of the Ministry of Education, if the building is registered by the Ministry;
   (b) the representative of the Committee for Religious Matters at the appropriate city or district soviet;
   (c) the representative of the religious association.

49. The decision of the technical committee stated in the examination document is binding and subject to execution.

50. If the technical committee decides that the building threatens to collapse, the committee must also indicate whether the building shall be demolished or made safe if appropriate repairs are made. In such case, the [examination] document shall describe in detail the necessary repairs for the prayer building and the date of completion. The religious association may not hold prayer or other meetings in the building until the repair work has been completed.

51. If the believers refuse to carry out the repairs as indicated in the [examination] document of the technical committee, the contract for the use of the building and religious property shall be annulled according to the decision of the [Council of Ministers] of the autonomous republic or oblast.

52. If, as required by the decision of the technical committee, the building shall be demolished, the contract for the use of the building and religious property shall be annulled according to the decision of the [Council of Ministers] of the autonomous republic or oblast.

53. [Any decision for the demolition of the prayer building] shall be carried out by the Committee for Religious Matters at the city or district soviet and the expenses defrayed from the sale of building material remaining after the demolition of the building. Any money left over shall be transferred to the Treasury.

54. The members of the groups of believers and religious societies may pool money in the prayer building or premises and outside it by voluntary collections and donations, but only among the members of the given religious association and only for the purpose of covering the expenses for the maintenance of prayer building or premises and religious property, and for the salary of the clergy and activities of the executive bodies.

Any kind of compulsory collection of money for the benefit of religious associations is punishable under the provisions of the Criminal Code.

55. It is compulsory to enter in the inventory of religious property any kind of religious property, whether donated, or purchased with the money received through voluntary donations.

The donations made for the purpose of beautifying the prayer building or religious property shall be entered in the general inventory of the religious property which is in use by the religious association free of charge.

All other donations in kind made for indefinite purposes, as well as donations in money to cover the upkeep of prayer buildings (renovation, heating, etc.), or for the benefit of the clergy shall not be subject to entry in the inventory. The donations in money shall be entered by the cashier in the account book.

56. Expenditures of donated money may be carried out by the members of the executive body in connection with the purposes for which it is donated.

57. Prayer meetings of the believers who formed a society or group may be held, without notification to or permission of the authorities, in prayer buildings or specially adapted premises which comply with the technical and sanitary regulations.

Divine services may be performed in the premises not specially adapted for these purposes, if notification [is made] to the Committee for Religious Matters.

58. Any kind of religious ceremonies or rites or display of objects of the cult in the buildings belonging to the State, public, cooperative or private institutions or enterprises is prohibited.

Such prohibition does not apply to the performance of religious rites in hospitals and prisons in specially isolated rooms if requested by dangerously ill or dying persons, or to the performance of religious ceremonies in cemeteries and in crematoria.

59. A special permission [granted] for each case separately by the Committee for Religious Matters is required for the performance of religious processions as well as the performance of religious rites in the open air. An application for such permission must be submitted at least two weeks prior to the ceremony. Such permission is not required for religious services connected with funerals.

60. Permission is not required for religious processions which are an inevitable part of the divine service and are made only around the prayer building, provided they do not disturb normal street traffic.

61. A permission of the agency which concluded the contract for the use of property is necessary for each religious procession as well as the performance of religious ceremonies outside the place where the religious association is situated. Such permission may be granted only with the agreement of the executive committee of the place where the procession of performance of ceremonies is supposed to take place.

62. A record of the religious societies and groups of believers shall be kept by agencies which register the religious association (Art. 6).

63. The registration agencies of religious associations (Art. 6) submit data to the Committee for Religious Matters at the city and district soviets in accordance with the forms and within the period established by the Permanent Committee for Religious Matters at the [Council of Ministers].

64. Surveillance over the activities of religious associations, as well as over the maintenance of prayer buildings and property leased to religious associations, shall be exercised by registration agencies, and in rural areas by village soviets.

Application of the Laws of 1929 and 1932

Instructions of the People's Commissariat for the Interior of 1929

Instructions of the People's Commissariat for the Interior (*Instruktsiia narodnogo kommissariata vnutrennykh del*) on Rights and Obligations of Religious Associations (*O pravakh i obiazannostiakh religioznykh ob'edinenii*) of October 1, 1929.[1]

I. PURPOSE AND COMPOSITION

1. Citizens of the same cult, denomination, sect or doctrine who are 18 years of age or over may form religious societies or groups of believers for the joint satisfaction of their religious needs.
2. Believers who have formed a religious society or group may:
   (a) perform religious rites;
   (b) arrange prayer or general meetings of believers;
   (c) manage religious property;
   (d) conclude transactions of the civil law connected with the management of religious property and the performance of religious rites;
   (e) appoint clergymen for the performance of religious rites.
3. The religious associations may not:
   (a) create mutual credit societies, poorhouses, charity schools, hospices, dormitories for the poor, funeral funds, etc.;
   (b) establish cooperatives, producing unions, and, in general, use the property at their disposal for any purpose other than the satisfaction of religious needs;

---

[1] Translated from N. Orleanskii. *Zakon o religioznykh ob'edineniiakh R.S.F.S.R.* (The Law Concerning the Religious Associations of the R.S.F.S.R.). Moscow: 1930. According to the Law on the Permanent Central Committee and Local Committees of Religious Matters (*O postoiannoi tsentral'noi i mestnykh komissiiakh po rasamotreniiu religiozynkh voprosov*) of May 30, 1931; for matters relating to the administration of churches, special committees at the Council of Ministers and city and district soviets were organized which took over the activities formerly exercised by the People's Commissariat for the Interior. The Committee for Religious Matters at the Council of Ministers issued a new instruction on January 28, 1932, changing only the names of the authorities.

(c) give material help to members of the association;

(d) organize special prayer or other meetings for children, youth, and women;

(e) organize scriptural, literary, sewing, labor or other meetings, groups, circles, sections, or such for teaching religion;

(f) organize excursions and children's playgrounds;

(g) organize libraries and reading rooms;

(h) organize health resorts and medical care.

Religious societies and groups do not enjoy the rights of a legal entity.

4. The membership of a religious society or group of believers may include only citizens who reside:

(a) in the same city;

(b) in the same city and vicinity;

(c) in the same village; or

(d) in several villages of the same district (*raion*).

5. A citizen may be a member of one religious association (society or group) of believers.

Persons who belong to several religious associations may be prosecuted in accordance with [the Criminal Code].

A citizen who desires to be a member of a religious association must submit a written or oral application to the executive body of the religious society or group of believers.

Members shall be accepted by the executive body or general assembly of the religious society or group of believers.

6. The activities of clergymen, preachers, preceptors, etc., are restricted to the area where the members of religious associations reside and to the place where the prayer premises are located.

The activities of clergymen, preachers, preceptors, etc., who permanently serve two or several religious associations, are restricted to the area where the believers who are members of these religious associations permanently reside.

A clergyman, preacher, preceptor, etc., may start his activities only after the date when the information respecting him has been submitted by the religious society or group of believers to the registration agency.

II. FORMATION AND EXPENDITURE OF MEANS

7. Members of a religious society or group of believers may collect in the prayer building voluntary donations (by collection boxes or plates) among all persons present.

Excepting the prayer building collection, only voluntary donations may take place among the members of a given religious society or group of believers.

8. Collections of voluntary donations among persons who are not members of a given religious association may be carried out only if permission is granted in accordance with the Law on the Collection of Voluntary Donations (*Sobranie uzakonenii*, 1924, No. 8, Art. 81, and 1925, No. 52, Art. 388).

9. Religious associations may not establish compulsory membership fees, or introduce membership cards with monthly indications of donations.

Any kind of compulsory exaction of fees for the benefit of a religious association shall be subject to punishment under [the Criminal Code].

10. Religious associations may collect donations and spend them only for purposes connected with the maintenance of prayer buildings and religious property and for the performance of religious rites, as well as for renumeration to clergymen, watchmen and singers, the activities of executive bodies of religious societies or groups of believers, and executive bodies of religious conventions and conferences.

11. Pecuniary donations and donations in kind for the maintenance (renovation, heating, etc.) of prayer buildings or premises, or for the benefit of the clergy shall not be included in the inventory but may be spent by members of the executive body of a religious society or a representative of a group of believers.

Voluntary pecuniary donations shall be entered by the cashier in the account book.

Any kind of religious property, whether donated or purchased from voluntary donations, shall be entered in the inventory of the religious property.

Voluntary donations made in order to beautify the prayer building by adding a donated object, or in order to beautify the religious objects, shall be entered in the inventory of the religious property.

12. Executive bodies of religious conferences and conventions may receive voluntary donations, but they may not organize collections of voluntary donations or introduce any kind of compulsory fees or subscriptions.

Members of the executive bodies of religious conferences and conventions may spend donations received from believers and religious associations only for expenditures connected with the activities and needs of the executive body.

III. EXECUTIVE BODIES

13. For the execution of the functions connected with the management and use of religious property, as well as for outside representation, the religious association elects from among its members, at the general assembly of believers, by open ballot, an executive body:

(a) for a religious society—three members and two substitutes;

(b) for a group of believers—one representative and his substitute.

Individual members of the executive body of a religious society or group of believers may be removed by the registration agency.

14. Individual citizens who are members of the executive body of a religious society or representatives of a group of believers may conclude transactions in their own names involving the management and use of the religious property, such as contracts respecting the employment of watchmen, the supply of firewood, renovation of the building and religious property, acquisition of products and property for the performance of religious rites and ceremonies, and they may engage in other activities closely and directly connected with the doctrine and rites of the given religious cult as well as conclude contract respecting the rental of premises for prayer meetings.

15. A religious society or group of believers may elect at the general assembly from among its members an accounting committee of not more than three members and two substitutes for exercising control over religious property and money received through the collection of voluntary donations.

16. Local, republican, All-Russian and All-Union religious conferences and conventions may elect, from among their participants, executive bodies for the execution of decisions of the convention or conference.

Decisions and decrees of the religious conferences and conventions and their executive bodies may be carried out only by voluntary action of the believers.

17. Executive bodies of religious conferences and conventions do not enjoy the rights of legal entities, and in addition to this, they may not:

(a) possess by contract or otherwise any religious property, acquire by purchase, or rent premises for prayer meetings;

(b) conclude any kind of contracts or transactions.

18. The area of activities of the executive bodies of religious conventions and conferences is restricted to the place where the religious societies or groups united by convention or conference are situated.

19. Executive bodies of religious societies or groups, as well as those of religious conventions and conferences, may use solely for religious matters stamps, seals, and stationery with their names [imprinted]. Such stamps, seals and stationery may not include emblems or slogans established for Soviet government agencies.

20. All applications (statements, petitions, inquiries, etc.) of the religious associations to State authorities and responses to them are subject to the stamp duty with the exception of applications submitted to agencies of local soviets.

Complaints regarding abuses and illegal activities of authorities are free from stamp duty no matter to which office they are submitted.

IV. MEETINGS AND CONVENTIONS

21. Prayer meetings, of the believers who have formed a religious society or group in prayer buildings or premises especially adapted for this purpose and considered satisfactory as to technical and sanitary conditions, may be arranged without notification to or permission of authorities.

    Buildings and premises may be used after their inspection by the proper sanitary-technical committee whenever the representative of the Committee for Religious Matters and the fire brigade shall participate.

22. Prayer meetings, in premises which are not especially adapted for this purpose (e.g., dwelling houses), may be arranged only if permission for each separate case is granted by the proper authority.

    Believers who have formed a religious society or group may notify the authorities concerning a series of prayer meetings to be held within a period of one year.

    Believers who have not formed a society or group must notify authorities regarding each such prayer meeting separately.

23. Permission by the proper authorities is necessary for general assemblies of religious societies or groups.

24. The following shall be submitted in an application for the convocation of the assembly:
    (a) the time and location of the assembly and the approximate number of participants;
    (b) agenda of the assembly;
    (c) the family name, name and patronymic of the responsible organizer (or organizers) of the assembly.

    A receipt shall be given to the organizer by request upon the acceptance of the application if it fulfills the requirements mentioned above.

25. The application shall be submitted in writing:
    (a) at least three days prior to the proposed prayer meeting;
    (b) at least two weeks prior to the proposed general assembly.

26. Information on the granting of permission or the denial of permission shall be transmitted to the organizer within seven days from the date of the submission of the application or, at any rate, no later than 24 hours prior to the proposed meeting or assembly.

27. Meetings of executive bodies and accounting committees of groups of believers or religious societies may be convoked without notice to or permission of the authorities.

28. The following may initiate and organize the convocation of a religious convention or conference: religious societies or groups of believers and their executive bodies as well as executive bodies of religious conventions and conferences.

    The following data shall be submitted in the application for granting the permission for the convocation of the convention or conference:
    (a) the time and location of the convention or conference;
    (b) the number of delegates to the convention or conference;
    (c) the territory covered by the convention or conference;
    (d) list of items subject to discussion in the convention or conference;
    (e) the family name, race, patronymic, profession and residence of the responsible organizer or organizers of the convention or conference.

    A receipt to the organizer shall be given at his request upon the acceptance of the application if it fulfills the requirements.

29. Permissions for local, All-Russian and All-Union conventions or conferences may be granted:
    (a) by the Permanent Committee for Religious Matters at the Council of Ministers in case an All-Russian or All-Union convention or conference is proposed to be convoked;
    (b) by the local Committee for Religious Matters if a local convention or conference is proposed to be convoked.

    Permission for the convocation of a republican convention or conference shall be granted by the Committee for Religious Matters of the appropriate republic.

30. The application for permission of the convocation of a local or republican convention or conference shall be submitted at least one month prior to the proposed meeting, and of the All-Russian or All-Union conference or convention, at least, two months prior to the proposed meeting.

    The responsible organizer shall be informed within two weeks of the decision on the granting or denial of permission for the convocation of a local or republican convention or conference, and of the convocation of an All-Russian or All-Union convention or conference within one month from the date of submission of the application.

31. Permission shall be denied if, according to its goal and the items on the agenda and the composition of the organizers or participants, the meeting, convention or conference is in conflict with the laws in effect in the territory of the R.S.F.S.R., threatens the social order and safety, or provokes discord and hostilities among the nations.

32. If a meeting, convention or conference for which permission is required was arranged without permission, the persons organizing or convoking such a meeting, convention or conference shall be prosecuted in court.

V. PROCESSIONS AND CEREMONIES

33. Any kind of religious rites or ceremonies or display of objects of a cult in the premises of State, public, cooperative or private institutions and enterprises shall be prohibited.

    This prohibition shall not apply to:

    (a) the performance of religious rites on the request of dying or dangerously ill persons in hospitals and prisons, if such rites or ceremonies are performed in specially isolated rooms, or to the performance of religious rites and ceremonies in cemeteries and crematoria;

    (b) images of religious characters (statues and pictures) of artistic, historic or museum value which are exhibited in museums, galleries and other similar institutions.

34. Any kind of religious ceremonies, such as prayers, requiem masses, baptisms, the bringing of holy images (*ikoni*), and the like, may be performed within the family or in apartments without the permission of or notification to authorities.

    The performance of religious rites may take place only if all persons living in rooms used in common are agreeable respecting the performance of such rites.

35. Permission of authorities is not required for religious processions which are an inevitable part of a divine service and are made only around the prayer building, providing they do not disturb street traffic.

36. Special permission, for each case separately, of the Committee for Religious Matters is required for the staging of religious processions as well as for the performance of religious rites outdoors.

    Permission is not required for religious services connected with a funeral.

37. The performance of religious rites as well as religious processions outside the place where the religious association is situated may be allowed by special permission, separately given for each case, issued by the agency which concluded the contract on the use of the religious property. Such permission may be issued only if the executive committee of the district in which the procession, rites or ceremonies are supposed to be performed is agreeable to such performance.

38. The application requesting permission for religious processions or ceremonies shall be submitted by organizers in writing at least two weeks prior to the proposed procession or ceremonies.

    The application must contain the following data:

(a) the purpose of the procession or ceremony;
(b) date and hour of the beginning of the procession and its duration;
(c) detailed route of the procession;
(d) supposed number of participants;
(e) the family name, name, patronymic, profession and residence of the responsible organizer or organizers.

A receipt shall be given to the organizer at his request upon the acceptance of the application.

The decision on the granting or denial of permission for the performance of the procession or ceremony shall be transmitted to the responsible organizer within three days prior to the proposed procession or ceremony.

39. Permission shall be denied if the procession or ceremony is contrary to the laws in effect, provokes discord or hostilities among nations, threatens the social order or safety or may disturb street traffic.

40. For each procession or ceremony, there shall be a responsible master of ceremonies who is obliged to keep order during the procession or ceremony, observe that street traffic is not disturbed, and prevent any deviation from the purpose or route of the procession or ceremony as indicated in the permission.

41. If a procession or ceremony for which permission is required was organized without such permission and was not discontinued according to the demand of the administrative authorities, the persons organizing such procession or ceremony shall be prosecuted in court.

VI. REGISTRATION

42. The local religious associations of believers who are 18 years of age or over shall be registered as religious societies or groups of believers.

No religious society may be organized with less than 20 citizens; however, a group of believers may be organized by citizens too few in number to organize a religious society.

43. A religious society or group of believers may start its activities only after registration by the Committee for Religious Matters at the proper city or district soviet.

44. The founders of a religious society or group of believers must submit two copies for registration:
(a) the application according to established form;
(b) the list of founders of the group of believers, or of not less than 20 of a religious society, according to the established form.

A receipt shall be given to the founders at their request upon the acceptance of the application, if it fulfills the requirements.

Persons who submit false data in the application for registration shall be prosecuted according to the provisions [of the Criminal Code].

45. The registration agencies must register the religious society or group of believers or advise the founders of the denial of the registration within one month from the date of the submission of the application.

46. The registration of a religious society or group of believers must be denied if its methods and forms of activities are contrary to the laws in effect, threaten the public order or safety, or provoke discord or hostilities among the nations.

VII. ACCOUNTING

47. A list of members of the executive bodies and accounting committees as well as a report on changes in this list shall be submitted within seven days by the religious society or group of believers to registration agencies.

Such a list and report shall be submitted in two copies according to the established form.

A receipt shall be given to the religious society or group of believers according to the established form upon acceptance of the list or report.

48. Data on the clergy, preachers, preceptors, etc., who serve the religious society or group of believers shall be submitted to the registration agency in two copies according to the established form.

    A receipt shall be given according to the established form upon acceptance of the date.

49. A religious association must submit to the registration agency a list of its members according to the established form.

    The first list shall include all members of the religious society or group of believers. By January 1 of each year, a report shall be submitted on changes in the list of members of the society or group.

50. If the provisions of the present instruction on the submission of data or reports are continuously violated by the religious society or group of believers, the registration agency may require the removal of the members of the executive body and the election of new members.

51. The materials of the religious convention or conference (records, decisions, reports) shall be submitted in two copies in accordance with the established form to the authority granting the permission for the convention or conference, together with the list of members of the elected executive body.

    A receipt shall be given in accordance with the established form upon the acceptance of the materials and the list of members of the executive body.

52. Records on the religious societies and groups of believers shall be kept by the registration agencies.

53. The registration agencies shall submit, in accordance with the form established by the Committee for Religious Matters, the data on religious associations to higher authorities.

VIII. SURVEILLANCE

54. The activities of the religious societies and groups of believers are under the surveillance of the proper committee for religious matters.

55. In exercising surveillance, the proper committee for religious matters, as well as other authorities whose duty it is to safeguard the revolutionary order and safety, may send their representatives to each assembly or meeting of believers for the purpose of watching over order and safety.

    Persons sent to the assembly for supervision over order and safety may not participate in discussions or voting or engage in the leading of the assembly.

56. Persons sent to the assembly for supervision over order and safety are obliged to adjourn the assembly:

    (a) in case of forcible activities of one part of the assembly toward another;

    (b) in case of any deviation from the agenda submitted by the organizers of the assembly, violation of order, or inciting to the commission of crimes or infringements of the law, if such activities were not stopped by the presidium or if the presidium, on the request of the person sent to the assembly did not adjourn the assembly;

    (c) if the presidium of the assembly asks collaboration of the person sent to the assembly to adjourn the assembly which deviated from the provisions of the law.

    The participants of the assembly declared adjourned must depart without delay. Persons failing to follow this demand shall be prosecuted.

57. Members of the militia, as well as the members of the local soviet, shall see to it that no forcible activities against persons are committed, no property demolished or abused, or other illegal activities performed during the processions and ceremonies.

58. Members of the militia, as well as local soviets and other authorities whose duty it is to safeguard the revolutionary order and safety, may send their representatives to any procession and ceremony for the maintenance of order and safety during the procession or ceremony.

    Persons sent to the procession or ceremony for maintaining order and safety may break off the procession if the lawful orders of authorities are not observed and demand that the participants depart without delay.

59. Inspection of religious societies and groups of believers shall be performed, if necessary, by committees for religious matters at the city or district soviets.

The inspection of executive bodies of religious conventions and conferences shall be performed by the Committee for Religious Matters at the Council of Ministers.

Files and records, as well as money matters, shall be examined during the inspection.

IX. LIQUIDATION

60. A religious society or group of believers may be liquidated in accordance with the decision of the general assembly of the society or group.

The registration agency shall be informed within seven days regarding such decision.

61. In case of a disclosure in the activities of a religious association of deviations from the rules established for such associations the registration agency shall demand the correction of the defects by the date indicated by the agency.

If the religious society or group of believers refuses to correct the defects, as well as in the case of the disclosure of the violation of laws, the city or district committee for religious matters may ask the Committee for Religious Matters at the Council of Ministers to liquidate the society or group.

Such a decision shall be delivered to the executive body of the society or group.

62. The decision on the liquidation of the religious society or group of believers may be appealed before the Council of Ministers within two weeks from the date of the delivery of the decision.

In case of an appeal, the religious society or group of believers shall be liquidated only after the confirmation of the decision.

Liquidation of the religious society or group of believers shall be executed by the committee for religious matters at the city or district soviet.

63. The contract leasing the prayer building and religious property for the use of believers free of charge may be annulled according to the decision of the Committee for Religious Matters at the Council of Ministers on the proposal of such Committee at the city or district soviet.

Believers who are members of the religious society or group shall be informed of such a decision.

64. The contract may be annulled if the religious association has not observed orders of authorities (on re-registration, renovation, etc.), as well as in the case when the prayer building is needed for State or public use.

65. If the believers who are members of the religious society or group, within two weeks from the date of announcement of the decision on the liquidation of the prayer building, take an appeal before the Council of Ministers, the contract shall be annulled, and the believers shall be deprived of the use of the building only after the confirmation of the decision.

The liquidation shall be carried out by the committee for religious matters at the city or district soviet in the presence of the representative of the finance department and other authorities interested in the case as well as of the representatives of the religious association.

Regulations of 1945

Situation of the Administration of the Church
The Forty-Eight Paragraphs[1]

*Adopted by the Provincial Sobor of the Russian
Orthodox Church January 31, 1945*

PROLOGUE

Within the Russian Orthodox Church the higher authority in the area of religious teaching, church administration and church justice—legislative, administrative, judicial—belongs to the Provincial Sobor, convened periodically and composed of bishops, clergy, and laymen.

PART I

Patriarch

1. In conformity with the 34th Canon of the Apostolic Canons[2] the Russian Orthodox Church is headed by his Holiness Patriarch of Moscow and All-Russia and is administered by him together with the Holy Synod.
2. The name of the Patriarch is mentioned at Divine Services in all churches of the Russian Orthodox Church in the U.S.S.R., also beyond the borders, by the following formula: "Of our Holy Father (name), Patriarch of Moscow and All Russia."
3. To the Patriarch belongs the right to appeal in pastoral addresses to the whole Russian Orthodox Church regarding church questions.
4. The Patriarch, in the name of the Russian Orthodox Church, carries on contacts concerning church matters with representatives of other autocephalous Orthodox Churches.

[1] "Polozhenie ob upravlenii russkoi pravoslavnoi tzerkvi," *Pravoslavni tzerkovni kalendar na 1946 god* (Moscow: The Moscow Patriarchate, 1946), pp. 58–60.
[2] "The bishops of every nation must acknowledge him who is first among them and account him as their head, and do nothing of consequence without his consent: but each may do those things only which concern his own parish, and the country places which belong to it. But neither let him 'who is the first' do anything without the consent of all, for so there will be unanimity, and God will be glorified through the Lord in the Holy Spirit." Scholars are generally in agreement that "there is good reason for assigning it (the canon) a date no later than the middle of the fourth century." *The Nicene and Post Nicene Fathers*, Vol. XIV: *The Seven Ecumenical Councils (2d series:* Grand Rapids: W. B. Eerdmans Publishing Co., 1956), pp. 591, 596.

5. The Patriarch, in case of need, gives to members of the hierarchy brotherly counsel and directives related to their duties and administration.
6. The Patriarch has the right to give promotions (elevation) to the members of the hierarchy according to the established titles and higher church distinctions.
7. The Patriarch in order to solve visibly important church questions convokes with the permission of the government a Sobor of Bishops and presides at the Sobor, but when it is necessary to hear out the voice of the clergy and laymen and there is the external possibility to convoke a regular Provincial Sobor, he convokes such and presides at it.
8. The Patriarch is the Diocesan[3] Hierarch of the Moscow Diocese.[4]
9. By the direction of the Patriarch, a Patriarchal Deputy with the title of Metropolitan of Krutitsk shall be granted full rights of Diocesan hierarch and is sanctioned to aid the Patriarch in administering general church matters of the Moscow Diocese.
10. Under immediate direction of the Patriarch of Moscow are the theological institutes—higher spiritual educational institutions, having the purposes of conveying spiritual education to the future pastors of the church and the preparation of instructors for the teaching of theological subject matter.
11. Concerning questions, demanding decision of the Government of the U.S.S.R., the Patriarch communicates with the Soviet on matters of the Russian Orthodox Church at the SNK[5] of the U.S.S.R.
12. In case of the death of the Patriarch or for other reasons making it impossible for him to fulfill the office of patriarchal obligations, the senior bishop by date of ordination who is also a permanent member of the Holy Synod becomes the Locum Tenens[6] of the Patriarchal throne.
13. During the interim period of Patriarchs:
    (a) the right of administration of the Russian Orthodox Church belongs to the Locum Tenens with the Holy Synod;
    (b) the name of the Locum Tenens is mentioned at Divine Services in all Russian Churches;
    (c) addresses to all Russian Churches, and to all representatives of autocephalous churches, come with the signature of the Patriarchal Locum Tenens;
    (d) the Metropolitan of Krutitsk administers independently the Moscow Diocese.
14. After the vacancy of the Patriarchal throne, the Holy Synod under the presidency of the Locum Tenens raises the question of convoking a Sobor for the selection of a new Patriarch and designates a time for the convocation which is to be no later than six months after the vacancy of the Patriarchal throne.
15. At the Sobor convoked for the selection of a Patriarch, the Locum Tenens presides.
16. The Patriarch has a seal and a stamp which are registered with the appropriate government authority.

PART II

Holy Synod

17. The Holy Synod consists of six members who are diocesan hierarchs. The President is the Patriarch.
18. Three members of the Holy Synod are permanent members, three are temporary.

[3] Eparchial.
[4] Eparchy.
[5] SNK-Sovnarkom-Sovet Narodnikh Kommissarov, Council of Ministers.
[6] Temporarily the real occupant.

19. Permanent members of the Holy Synod are the Metropolitans: Kiev, Leningrad, and Krutitsk.
20. The temporary members of the Synod are called to attend one session. They are selected from the list of hierarchs according to the date of ordination. One is selected from each group, into which all dioceses are separated.
21. The Synodical Year is divided into two sessions: summer session (March-August) and winter session (September-February).
22. For the management of separate spheres under the administration of the Patriarchate, separate departments (education, publication, economic, and others) may be organized by the Holy Synod.

PART III

Dioceses

23. The Russian Orthodox Church is divided into dioceses, the borders of which must correspond with the government borders[7]—districts, regions, and republics.
24. At the head of a diocese, stands the Diocesan Hierarch, who carries the title of his cathedral city, and is appointed by Decree of his Beatitude the Patriarch.
25. Vicar bishops are appointed by the Diocesan Hierarch at his discretion. Their duties are determined by the Diocesan Hierarch.
26. The Diocesan Hierarch is the responsible head of his diocese which he administers either personally "under local conditions" or through the participation of a Diocesan Council utilizing his responsible stamp and seal which is registered under the government authority. Each hierarch has a Diocesan Hierarchal Chancery.
27. The Diocesan Council, where there is such constituted by the Hierarch, consists of three to five persons of presbyter rank. The mission of the Diocesan Council is to prepare for hierarchal decision matters sent to them for this purpose by the Diocesan Hierarch.
28. The Diocesan Hierarch has the right of appeal with hierarchal messages within the boundary of his diocese.
29. The diocese is divided into deaneries, headed by a dean, appointed by the Diocesan Hierarch.
30. The dean oversees the activities and conduct of the parish clergy of the area; visiting the parishes no less than twice a year; announcing the decisions of the Diocesan Hierarch; in case of need, giving brotherly direction to the parish rector and to other clerics; concerning himself about satisfying the religious need of the faithful of a parish which at the time has no clergy; interceding before the hierarch for the elevation of those deserving stimulation; and submitting a semi-annual report of his activities on the area entrusted to him by the Diocesan Hierarch; reporting without delay about particularly important incidents and also overseeing the correctness of the management of the parishes.
31. Once a year on a designated form the Diocesan Hierarch submits a report to the Patriarch about the diocese entrusted to him.
32. In the diocese where it is possible and with permission of the particular organs of authority, theological-pastoral courses for the preparation of candidates for the priesthood are created in accordance with programs adopted by the Patriarch.
33. In order to insure that the churches of the diocese have the items essential to the Divine Services—church candles, incense, etc., the diocese, with permission of the local government authorities, may establish candle factories and places for the preparation of crowns, crosses, prayers of absolution and similar items.
34. Monasteries in the diocese are governed by the regulations adopted by the Patriarch.

  [7] *Oblastnimi, kraievimi i respublikanskimi.*

PART IV

Parishes

35. At the head of every parish society of believers stands the rector of the parish, appointed by the Diocesan Hierarch for the spiritual guidance of the faithful and the governing of the clerics and parish.

36. The rector of the parish is responsible to the Diocesan Hierarch for fulfilling in accordance with church rubrics the serving of Divine Services, the exact fulfillment of the directives of the Diocesan Hierarchs dealing with the spiritual guidance of the staff and the parish society. The rectors of the church are especially obligated to see that the tenor and order of parish life does not hinder the parishioners from fulfilling their duties as citizens. For example: in village areas, Divine Services are to be conducted only during the hours not scheduled for village communal work, etc. This is important during periods of field work.

37. The parish society may be organized by the voluntary agreement of believers only after its registration with the local government authorities on the basis of submitted intention.

38. The leasing of church buildings or prayer homes to a parish society of believers comes about in answer to their intention under the authority of the organ of the government with the agreement of the Diocesan Hierarch, who oversees the expediency or advisability of the distribution of the churches and parishes in his diocese.

39. The Orthodox parish society, a unit of believers, "not less than twenty persons," receives free use of a church assigned to it and objects destined for the rite from the local government authority by special agreement, which holds the group responsible for overseeing and protecting these church properties. An executive body is composed from its midst of three persons and the rector of the parish, who are responsible with those who signed the agreement for proper utilization of all properties before the civil authorities.

40. The rector of the parish as a result of his functions is an incontrovertible member of the parish society and he is the president of its executive organ "church council." This consists of four members. In addition to the rector those responsible are the parish elder, his assistant, and the treasurer. (All three are elected at a general parish meeting or, if a parish society is reorganizing, they are elected from the midst of a group of believers who receive the free use of the church).

41. The executive body of the parish society of believers is under the immediate guidance and supervision of the rector of the church and is responsible before civil authorities for the preservation of the buildings and properties of the church. It directs church management and is concerned about salaries, heating, lighting, and repair of the church and objects destined for the rite; it is concerned about supplies which are essential for the performance of the Divine Service within the church such as: vestments, devotional books, incense, burial emblems, forgiveness (burial) prayers, neck crosses, and so forth; it pays the necessary amounts for receiving the Holy Chrism through the Diocesan Hierarch from the Patriarchate; it is the responsible decision maker on financial matters of the parish, maintaining correct accounts of receipts and expenses; it makes contributions and divisions of the parish funds for church and patriotic needs and for support of the staff if by agreement the staff is to receive for its efforts a given salary from the parish; it pays the necessary amounts for support of the Diocesan Hierarch and his administration for Diocesan theological-pastoral courses, and for general church needs such as the Patriarchal Administration and for the support of Spiritual Educational Institutions at the Patriarchate.

42. The general parish meeting selects an Auditing Committee composed of three persons. The auditing committee of the parish society has permanent responsibility of looking after the condition of the church property and the movable church money. Once every quarter it is to accomplish a documentary

auditing of church properties and money. It is to verify the entries of expenses, and to submit its decisions and recommendations to the attention of the general meeting of parishoners or group of believers which has received the free use of the church. In case of abuse and shortage of property or financial means, the auditing committee prepares a report and forwards it to the Gorsovet (City Council) or the Sel'sovet (Village Council).

43. The church money consists of: voluntary contributions of the believers by plate offerings at Divine Services, contributions made for altar bread, candles, etc., and general offerings made for church needs.

44. The church's money is deposited for safe keeping in a bank or savings account in the name of the given church and is drawn out by check signed by the rector and treasurer of the parish. The parish sums are entered in a parish ledger.

45. Information concerning income and expense is submitted semi-annually to the Diocesan Hierarch by the rector.

46. In case of unlawful acts by all or separate members of the executive body, the rector of the parish submits a report to the Diocesan Hierarch who by immediate investigation or through the dean and in communication with the Authoritative Soviet on matters of the Russian Orthodox Church at the SNK of the U.S.S.R., recommends to the group to replace the erring members of the executive body with new persons.

47. In case of the rector's death or his transfer to another parish, the executive body composes an act of an inventory of church holdings. The new rector enters in agreement with the local executive organ supervising these holdings.

48. The rector of the parish has his own seal and stamp registered with the appropriate government authority.

Regulations of 1961

Situation of the Administration of the Church
The Forty-Eight Paragraphs as Amended in 1961[1]

Changes resulting from the Sobor of Hierarchs which was convened by Patriarch Alexei at the Troitski-Sergeivska Lavra (Zagorsk) on July 18, 1961.

PART I
Concerning the Patriarch

No changes.

PART II
Concerning the Holy Synod

No. 18—Five members of the Holy Synod are permanent members (instead of three); three are temporary.
No. 19—Permanent members of the Holy Synod are the Metropolitans: Kiev, Leningrad, and Krutitsk; the bishop who administers the Moscow Diocese; and the bishop who presides over the External Church Affairs Department of the Moscow Patriarchate.

PART III
Concerning the Dioceses

No. 30—Eliminate the phrase after the last comma ("and also overseeing the correctness of the management of the parishes").

PART IV
Concerning the Parishes

The whole section relating to the administration of parishes is replaced by eleven new articles; Article 43 remains as it was. The articles about the rector which are not related to the administration of the parish, such as: Articles 47 and 48, as stated in this section concerning parishes remain the same as in the 1945 regulations.

[1] *Zhurnal*, No. 8, 1961, pp. 5–17.

Parishes

1. The Orthodox parish society of the Russian Orthodox Church consists of no less than twenty Orthodox believers under canonical guidance of a bishop and created by the voluntary agreement of the believers for the satisfying of religious-moral needs under the spiritual guidance of a priest selected by the group. Having received the blessing of the Diocesan Hierarch and being registered by the local government authority, and having received from the local civil authority free use of the church and objects destined for the rite, by agreement is completely answerable for the proper utilization of all properties in accordance with the Soviet laws.

2. The parish society is a part of the Russian Orthodox Church and of the Ecumenical Church of Christ, and has an independent character as regards management and finances.

3. For the management of parish matters and in conjunction with the general church conciliatory administration, two agencies are organized: the church parish meeting as an organ of decision and order (meeting of members and the twenty founders), and the church parish soviet as an executive body, consisting of three persons—an elder, assistant to the elder, and a treasurer, elected by the society from parishioners who are capable and of good Christian morals.

   For the continual overseeing of the condition of the Church property and current financial sums; for the preparation of quarterly documental audits; and for the examination of expenditures and receipts, an audit committee of three persons is elected and submits its findings and recommendations for review at the general parish meeting.

   In case of finding any abuse or shortage in matters of property or funds, the auditing committee prepares a report and forwards it to the local city council or village council.

4. The parish meeting, composed of those who had concluded agreement for use of the church and the cult property, is called when necessary with the permission of the local city or regional council (in village locals) and decides all matters concerning the administration and life of those societies.

5. The executive body of the parish society of believers is responsible for its activities to the general parish meeting, administers the management-financial life of the parish in the period between the two parish meetings. It carries the responsibility before the civil authorities for the protection of the buildings and the properties of the church. It directs church management and concerns itself about salary, heating, lighting, and repairing of the church, and objects destined for the rite and supplies which are essential for the performance of divine services within the church, such as: vestments, devotional books, incense, burial emblems, forgiveness (burial) prayers, neck crosses, and so forth. The executive body is the responsible decision maker about the financial matters of the parish. It maintains correct accounts of receipts and expenses. It makes contributions and division of the parish funds for church and patriotic needs; pays for support of church servers, if such are hired, according to a fixed salary; supports the workers and servers of the parish; it contributes voluntary amounts for the support of the Diocesan Hierarch and his administration and for the Patriarchal Administration and the support of spiritual-educational institutions at the Patriarchate; and into the pension fund, coming out of the needs and according to the funds on hand received from the free will contribution of the believers for the church needs.

6. Paragraph 43 of the Forty-Eight Paragraphs remains the same.

7. The income of the religious society is deposited for safekeeping in a government bank in the name of the given society and is drawn out by check signed by the president (elder) and treasurer of the church soviet of the religious society. The capital funds of the group are entered in the income-expense ledger.

8. The executive body of the religious society has its own stamp and seal registered with the appropriate government authority.
9. The rector of the parish and the other priests (where there are such) are the pastors of the parish, to whom the bishop entrusts the fulfilling in the parish church communal Divine Services and church needs (stoles), the giving of church sacraments according to the Church Rubrics, and guiding the parish in Christian life. They are responsible before God and their own bishop for the good estate of the parish in the realm of its religious condition and moral attainments.
10. The rector of the church. remembering the words of the Apostle: "and we will give ourselves continually to prayer and to the ministry of the word" (Acts 6:2–4), translates into reality the *spiritual guidance* of his parishioners; sees to it that the Divine Services are performed in the church zealously, in splendor, in accordance with the demands of Church Rubrics; and that all of the religious needs of the parishioners are satisfied at the proper time and with thoroughness. He translates into reality and looks after the discipline of members of his staff and intercedes for them before his spiritual head for elevations. He concerns himself about the development of good morality in his parish. For the fulfillment of this purpose, he first of all gives a good example in his own personal conduct in the parish. He also concerns himself about the furnishings for the Divine Services that they are kept in satisfactory condition, and brings to the attention of the executive body of the society the needs which are related to the normal fulfillment of Divine Services, needs (stoles), and church sacraments.
11. The executive body does not interfere with the Divine Services and in matters involving the relationship of the staff to each other. In case of abnormality in these matters, it refers them to the bishop, to whom belongs the exclusive competence in making decisions in these matters.
    The psalmist, those serving in the church, altar, and in general those who in one way or another participate in the Divine Services are hired by the executive body for the specific duties with the consultation of the pastor.
12. Strict adherence by the clergy as well as the parish society to the government regulation concerning the Church, not to mention church discipline, is absolutely mandatory. The well-being of the Russian Orthodox Church and the parish in particular depends on this.
    (Basis: "Book of canons of the holy apostles, Ecumenical and Provincial Sobors of the holy fathers"; "Situation of the Administration of the Russian Orthodox Church" 1945; Journalistic Resolutions of the Holy Synod of the Russian Orthodox Church. April 18, 1961; Resolutions of the VCIK and SNK RSFSR "Concerning Religious Associations," April 8, 1929.)

Statement of Archbishop Andrei

Statement of Archbishop Andrei of Saratov[1]

Interview held on December 24, 1941 with Associated Press

From the Editors:
The author . . . Archbishop of Saratov, Andrei, held a lengthy talk on 24 December 1941 with Gilmore Eddy Layner King, a correspondent of the agency "Associated Press." The editorial board found it necessary to include that interview in this book.

Correspondent: In which way and to what extent is the church helping in the defense of the nation?
Archbishop: The Russian Church has never been remote to the great events affecting the nation. She always came to her aid. Now when terrible dangers have visited our homeland the Church again comes to aid the fatherland. She has intensified her prayers which seek the gift of victory over the spiteful and crafty enemy. She, represented by the first hierarch, Metropolitan Sergei, turned to the faithful and requested them all to stand in the defense of the homeland. Money for the defense fund and warm items for the fighters are being collected through the churches.
Correspondent: To what extent is there limitation of freedom to confessing of the faith?
Archbishop: The Soviet authorities never limited the freedom of confessing of the faith. The Soviet authorities hold steadfastly to the principle of religious toleration for all religions and that religious toleration has been made into law by a separate paragraph in the Constitution. The Soviet authorities did employ repressions against some of the clergy and faithful not because of their religious convictions but because of their activities which were directed against the existence of the Soviet system. It is important to keep in mind that until the revolution the church was in the service of the Czarist government and it had many privileges and outlets (especially the higher ranks of clergy).Thus, it was difficult for the clergy to part with these advantages. Others lived in hope that the Soviet authorities would be overthrown and they stepped out against them. It is understandable that the Soviet authorities could not leave such people without censure.
From this there was created in some foreign persons an image of a limiting of freedom of confession of faith by the Soviet authorities. To correctly understand this question it is necessary to keep clearly in mind the relationship of

[1] *Pravda o religii v Rossii* (Moscow: The Moscow Patriarchate, 1942), pp. 120-122.

the government to religion on the one hand, and the relationship of various social organizations which conduct anti-religious propaganda such as Union of Militant Godless and their relationship to religion on the other hand.

Correspondent: Have there been any changes in the situation of the church since the beginning of the war?

Archbishop: No changes have occurred because the church was not restricted in its activities before the war nor since the beginning of the war.

Correspondent: Do you assume that, after the victory over the enemies, the relationship between the church and the government will remain as it is at the present time or will it change? Will it become better or worse?

Archbishop: The relationship of the church and the Soviet authorities will remain the same after the victory. You see, even the clergy say that the Soviet authority never persecuted them for religious convictions. Consequently, it does not protest against the Soviet authority; therefore no changes can come about.

Correspondent: Some Catholic circles in America are equating the conditions of religion in Germany and in Russia.

Archbishop: The Catholics in the USA are led into error by information that the Soviet authority presumably interferes in religious matters. There is a great difference between the relationship of the Soviet authority toward religion and the relationship toward religion in fascist Germany. . .

Correspondent: What percent attend church at the present time?

Archbishop: In years of tension and general trouble the faithful await comfort from prayer in church; therefore, the church is especially full of worshippers.

Correspondent: What percent of servicemen attend church?

Archbishop: Servicemen attend church as rare individuals.

In all churches ceremonial molebens are offered for victory of our military and the military of those nations friendly with us. This particularly applies for victory of the military of America.

In conclusion Archbishop Andrei expressed hope that America, as a wealthy nation, where much gold is collected, will unmercenarily give brotherly assistance to its ally—Russia. Gilmore responded affirmatively.

BIBLIOGRAPHY

Bibliography

Much has been published since World War II on various aspects of the Soviet system. A selection has been made from these publications which may be read to advantage to supplement the material included in this book—especially the historical perspective. This list is concerned with the most recent and pertinent material. To assist the reader, publications in a foreign language are given in their original title with an English translation. A list of abbreviations and an explanation of terms are also included.

List of Abbreviations and Terms

A S S R—Autonomous Soviet Socialist Republic
Bolsheviks—From bol'shenstvo—majority of Russian Social-Democratic Labor Party, headed by Lenin.
Cheka—The Extraordinary Commission for the Struggle against Counter-Revolution; Speculation and Office Crimes. First of a series of titles for the Soviet secret political police.
Glavnauki—From, in charge of education.
Gorsovet—City Soviet.
G P U—State Political Administration. Another designation for the Soviet secret political police.
Ispolkom—Executive Committee.
Mensheviks—From menshenstvo—minority of Russian Social-Democratic Labor Party, headed by anti-Leninists.
N E P—New Economic Policy.
N K V D—Peoples' Commissariat of Internal Affairs. Another designation for the Soviet secret political police.
R S F S R—Russian Socialistic Federal Soviet Republic.
Sel'sovet—Village Soviet.
S N K—Council of Peoples' Commissars.
V C I K—The All-Russian Central Executive Committee. Also used as All-Russian C I K.

Books

Abraham, Gerald (ed.). *The Music of Tschaikovsky.* New York: W. W. Norton and Company, Inc., 1946.
Alexei, Patriarch Moskovski i vseia Russi. Slova, rechi, poslaniia i obrasheniia. [*Sermons, Speeches, Messages and Addresses*]. 3 vols. Moscow: The Moscow Patriarchate, 1948, 1954, 1957.

149

150   *Communist Russia and the Russian Orthodox Church, 1943–1962*

Anderson, Paul B. *People, Church and State in Modern Russia.* New York: The Macmillan Co., 1944.
Bach, Marcus. *God and the Soviets.* New York: Thomas Y. Crowell, 195ὁ.
Bales, James D. *Communism Its Faith and Fallacies.* Grand Rapids: Baker Book House, 1962.
Barron, J. B., and Waddams, H. H. *Communism and the Churches: A Documentation.* London: S. C. M. Press, Ltd., 1950.
Bauer, Raymond A., Inkeles, Alex, and Kluckhohn, Clyde. *How the Soviet System Works.* New York: Vintage Books, 1960.
Baynes, Norman H. *The Byzantine Empire.* London: Oxford University Press, 1952.
————. *Byzantine Studies and Other Essays.* London: The Athlone Press, 1955.
Beazley, Raymond, Forbes, Nevill, and Birkett, O. A. *Russia: From the Varangians to the Bolsheviks.* Oxford: The Clarendon Press, 1918.
Bell, Earl H. *Social Foundations of Human Behavior: Introduction to the Study of Sociology.* New York: Harper and Brothers, 1961.
Bennett, John C. *Christianity and Communism Today.* London: S. C. M. Press, Ltd., 1960.
Benz, Ernst. *The Eastern Orthodox Church: Its Thoughts and Life.* Translated by Richard Winston and Clara Winston. Garden City: Doubleday and Company, Inc., 1963.
Berdyaev, Nicholas. *The Origin of Russian Communism.* Translated by R. M. French. Ann Arbor: University of Michigan Press, 1955.
Bereday, George, and Penner, Joan (eds.). *The Politics of Soviet Education.* New York: Frederick A. Praeger, 1960.
Biblioteka, Skol'naia. *Ot mraka k svetu: antireligioznaia kniga dlia chteniia.* [*From Darkness Toward Light: Antireligious Book For Reading*]. Moscow: Detgiz, 1959.
Blair, M. M. *Christ, Christianity and Communism.* Cincinnati: The Standard Publishing Company, 1950.
Bogolepov, A. A. *Tzerkov pod vlastiiu kommunisma.* [*The Church Under Communist Authority*]. Munich: Institut po izucheniiù SSSR, 1958.
Bolshakoff, Serge. *The Christian Church and the Soviet State.* London: Society for the Promoting of Christian Knowledge, 1942.
————. *The Doctrine of the Unity of the Church.* London: S.P.C.K., 1946.
————. *Russian Nonconformity.* Philadelphia: The Westminster Press, 1950.
Booth, Alan. *Christians and Power Politics.* London: S. C. M. Press, Ltd., 1961.
Braun, Leopold L. *Religion in Russia: An Uncensored Account, From Lenin to Khrushchev.* Paterson: St. Anthony Guild Press, 1959.
Bredemeier, Harry C., and Stephenson, Richard M. *The Analysis of Social Systems.* New York: Holt, Rinehart and Winston, Inc., 1962.
Brian-Chaninov, Nicholas. *The Russian Church.* Translated by Warre B. Wells. New York: The Macmillan Co., 1930.
Bury, J. B. *A History of Freedom of Thought.* New York: Henry Holt and Company, 1913.
Buzek, Anthony. *How the Communist Press Works.* London: Pall Mall Press, 1964.
Cadoux, Cecil John. *The Early Church and the World.* Edinburgh: T. & T. Clark, 1955.
Cantril, Hadley. *Soviet Leaders and Mastery Over Men.* New Brunswick: Rutgers University Press, 1960.
Casey, Robert Pierce. *Religion in Russia.* New York: Harper and Brothers, 1946.
Cockburn, Hutchison, J. *Religious Freedom in Eastern Europe.* Richmond: John Knox Press, 1953.
Cooke, Richard J. *Religion in Russia Under the Soviets.* New York: The Abingdon Press, 1924.
Crankshaw, Edward. *Khrushchev's Russia.* Baltimore: Penguin Books, 1959.
Cronyn, George W. *A Primer on Communism: 200 Questions and Answers.* New York: E. P. Dutton and Co., Inc., 1961.
Cully, Kendig B. *Basic Writings in Christian Education.* Philadelphia: The Westminster Press, 1960.

Curtiss, John S. *Church and State in Russia*. New York: Columbia University Press, 1940.
————. *The Russian Church and the Soviet State*. Boston: Little, Brown and Co., 1953.
Daniels, Robert V. *A Documentary History of Communism*. 2 vols. New York: Vintage Press, 1962.
DeGrunwald, Constantin. *The Churches and the Soviet Union*. Translated by J. J. Robinson-Paskevsky. New York: The Macmillan Company, 1962.
DeKoster, Lester. *Communism and Christian Faith*. Grand Rapids: William B. Eerdmans Publishing Co., 1962.
Denisov, A., and Kirichenko, M. *Soviet State Law*. Translated by S. Belsky and M. Saifulin and edited by D. Ogden and M. Perelman. Moscow: Foreign Language Publishing House, 1960.
Deutscher, Isaac. *Stalin: A Political Biography*. New York: Vintage Books, 1960.
Dobroliubov, Nikolai A. *O religii i tzerkvi*. [*Concerning Religion and the Church*]. Moscow: Academy of Sciences, U.S.S.R., 1960.
Emeliiakh, L. I. *Proizhozdeniia hristianskoho kul'ta*. [*Origin of the Christian Cult*]. Moscow: Uzhizgiz, 1961.
Emhardt, William C. *Religion in Soviet Russia*. New York: Columbia University Press, 1929.
Evans, Stanley. *The Churches in the U.S.S.R.* London: Cobbet Publishing Co., Ltd., 1943.
Every, George. *The Byzantine Patriarchate: 451–1204*. London: S.P.C.K., 1962.
Fedotov, George P. *The Russian Religious Mind*. New York: Harper Torchbooks, 1946.
Feuer, Lewis S. (ed.). *Basic Writings on Politics and Philosophy: Karl Marx and Friedrich Engels*. New York: Anchor Books, 1959.
Frankland, Noble. *Imperial Tragedy: Nicholas II, Last of the Tsars*. New York: Coward-McCann, Inc., 1961.
French, R. M. *The Eastern Orthodox Church*. London: Gainsborough Press, 1951.
Frere, W. H. *Links in the Chain of Russian Church History*. London: Faith Press, 1951.
Fuller, Edmond (ed.). *The Christian Idea of Education*. New Haven: Yale University Press, 1958.
Gavin, Frank. *Some Aspects of Contemporary Greek Thought*. London: S.P.C.K., 1936.
Goode, William J., and Hatt, Paul K. *Methods in Social Research*. New York: McGraw-Hill Book Company, 1952.
Gorer, Geoffrey, and Rickman, John. *The People of Great Russia: A Psychological Study*. New York: W. W. Norton and Company, Inc., 1962.
Gorodetsky, Nadejda. *The Humiliated Christ in Modern Russia Thought*. London: S.P.C.K., 1938.
————. *Saint Tikhon Zadensky: Inspirer of Dostoevsky*. London: S.P.C.K., 1951.
Greenslade, S. L. *Church and State from Constantine to Theodosius*. London: S.C.M. Press, Ltd., 1954.
Gregori, Archimandrite (censor). *Prakticheskoe izlozhenie tzerkovnograzhdanskih postanovleniiu k rukovodstva sviashennika* [*Practical Collection of Church and Government Decisions for Guidance of a Priest*]. 7th ed., St. Petersburg: Synodal'naia Typografiia, 1890.
Gross, Feliks. *The Seizure of Political Power*. New York: Philosophical Library, 1958.
Gsovski, V. (ed.). *Church and State Behind the Iron Curtain*. New York: Frederick A. Praeger, 1955.
————. *Soviet Civil Law: Private Rights and Their Background under the Soviet Regime*. 2 vols. Ann Arbor: University of Michigan Law School, 1948.
Gustafson, Arfved. *The Catacomb Church*. Jordanville, N.Y.: Holy Trinity Monastery Press, 1960.
Healy, Martin J. *The Whole Story*. Brooklyn: Confraternity of the Precious Blood, 1959.

152   Communist Russia and the Russian Orthodox Church, 1943–1962

Hearst, Randolph W., Jr., Conniff, Frank, and Considine, Bob. *Khrushchev and the Russian Challenge.* New York: Avon Book Division, 1961.
Hecker, Julius F. *Religion under the Soviets.* New York: Vanguard Press, 1927.
———. *Religion and Communism.* London: Chapman and Hall Ltd., 1933.
Hindus, Maurice. *Humanity Uprooted.* Norwood: Plimpton Press, 1930.
Hingley, Ronald. *Under Soviet Skins.* London: Hamish Hamilton, 1961.
Homans, George Caspar. *The Human Group.* New York: Harcourt, Brace and Company, 1950.
———. *Social Behavior: Its Elementary Forms.* New York: Harcourt, Brace and World, Inc., 1961.
Hoover, J. Edgar. *Masters of Deceit.* New York: Pocket Books, Inc., 1961.
———. *A Study of Communism.* New York: Holt, Rinehart and Winston, Inc., 1962.
Horecky, Paul L. (ed.). *Basic Russian Publications: A Selected and Annotated Bibliography on Russia and the Soviet Union.* Chicago: The University of Chicago Press, 1962.
Hunt, Carew, R. N. *Books on Communism.* London: Clark, Doble and Brendon Ltd., 1959.
———. *Marxism Past and Present.* New York: The Macmillan Company, 1959.
———. *The Theory and Practice of Communism: An Introduction.* New York: The Macmillan Company, 1961.
Jacobs, Dan N. (ed.). *The Communist Manifesto and Related Documents.* Evanston: Row, Peterson and Company, 1961.
Jahoda, Marie, Deutsch, Morton, and Cook, Stuart W. *Research Methods in Social Relations: With Special Reference to Prejudice.* 2 vols. New York: The Dryden Press, 1958.
Keller, Adolf. *Christian Europe Today.* New York: Harper and Brothers, 1942.
———. *Church and State on the European Continent.* Chicago: Willet Clark and Co., 1936.
Kerensky, A. F. *The Prelude to Bolshevism.* New York: Dodd, Mead and Company, 1919.
Kirchner, Walter. *History of Russia.* New York: Barnes and Noble, Inc., 1957.
Kluckhohn, Frank L. *The Naked Rise of Communism.* Derby: Monarch Books, Inc., 1962.
Kolarz, Walter. *Religion in the Soviet Union.* London: Macmillan and Co., Ltd., 1961.
Kulski, Wladyslaw W. *Peaceful Co-Existence: An Analysis of Soviet Foreign Policy.* Chicago: Henry Regnery Company, 1959.
———. *The Soviet Regime.* Syracuse: Syracuse University Press, 1959.
Leighton, Alexander H. *The Governing of Men.* Princeton: Princeton University Press, 1950.
Leipman, Heinz. *Rasputin and the Fall of Imperial Russia.* New York: Robert M. McBride Co., Inc., 1959.
Leonhard, Wolfgang. *Child of the Revolution.* Translated by C. M. Woodhouse. Chicago: Henry Regnery Company, 1958.
Loomis, Charles P., and Beegle, J. Allan. *Rural Sociology: The Strategy of Change.* Englewood Cliffs, N.J.: Prentice-Hall, Inc., 1957.
Lowrie, Charles W. *Communism and Christ.* New York: Morehouse-Gorham Co., 1952.
Lowrie, Donald A. *The Light of Russia.* Prague: The Y.M.C.A. Press Ltd., 1923.
McCullagh, Capt. Francis. *The Bolshevik Persecution of Christianity.* London: Billings and Son, Ltd., 1924.
Mackenzie, F. A. *The Russian Crucifixion.* London: The Gainsborough Press, 1930.
Mager, N. H., and Katel, Jacques. *Conquest Without War.* New York: Pocket Books, Inc., 1961.
Maughan, Hamilton H. *The Liturgy of the Eastern Orthodox Church.* London: Faith Press, 1916.
Mayo, Henry B. *Introduction to Marxist Theory.* 2d ed. New York: Oxford University Press, 1960.

Meerloo, Joast A. N. *The Rape of the Mind*. New York: Grosset and Dunlap, 1961.

Merzliukin, A. S. *O katolicheskom dogmate 1854 goda: O zachatie neporochnoi Devi Marii. [Concerning the Catholic Dogma of 1854: Regarding the Immaculate Conception of the Virgin Mary]*. Paris: No publisher given, 1960.

Meyendorff, John. *The Orthodox Church: Its Past and its Role in the World Today*. Translated by John Chapin. New York: Pantheon Books, 1962.

Miliukov, Paul. *Outlines of Russian Culture*. Edited by Michael Karpovich and translated by Valentine Ughet and Eleanor Davis. 3d ed. Philadelphia: University of Pennsylvania Press, 1948.

Miller-Fulop, Rene. *Rasputin the Holy Devil*. Garden City: Garden City Publishing Company, Inc., 1928.

Miller, William J., Roberts, Henry L., and Shulman, Marshall D. *The Meaning of Communism*. Morristown: Silver Burdett Company/Time Incorporated, 1963.

Mirsky, D. S. *Russia: A Social History*. London: The Cresset Press, 1952.

Moffatt, James. *The First Five Centuries of the Church*. London: University of London Press, Ltd., 1938.

Monastery, Holy Trinity. *Tzarskaia rossiia i vostochniia patriarchi. [Czarist Russia and the Eastern Patriarchs]*. Jordanville, N.Y.: Holy Trinity Printing Press, 1961.

Monnerot, Jules. *Sociology and Psychology of Communism*. Translated by Jane Degras and Richard Rees. Boston: Beacon Press, 1960.

Moore, Barrington, Jr. *Soviet Politics: The Dilemma of Power*. Cambridge: Harvard University Press, 1959.

————. *Terror and Progress in the U.S.S.R.* Cambridge: Harvard University Press, 1954.

Mosely, Philip E. *The Kremlin and World Politics: Studies in Soviet Policy and Action*. New York: Vintage Books, 1960.

Mouravieff, A. N. *A History of the Church of Russia*. Translated by R. W. Blackmore. Oxford: John Henry Parker, 1842.

Moxon, Allen T. *St. Chrysostom on the Priesthood*. London: S.P.C.K., 1932.

Murray, Victor A. *The State and Church in a Free Society*. Cambridge: The University Press, 1958.

Nahimov, Nikolai (ed.). *Vera, molitva i zhisn. [Faith, Prayer and Life]*. St. Petersburg: Sel'skaho Vestnika, 1912.

Nicholas, Metropolitan. *Speeches on Peace: Third Series 1955–1957*. Moscow: The Moscow Patriarchate, 1958.

Niebuhr, Richard H. *The Purpose of the Church and its Ministry*. New York: Harper and Brothers, 1956.

Niebuhr, Richard H., and Williams, Daniel D. (eds.). *The Ministry in Historical Perspective*. New York: Harper and Brothers, 1956.

Niebuhr, Richard H., Williams, Daniel D., and Gustafson, James M. *The Advancement of Theological Education*. New York: Harper and Brothers, 1957.

Nikolai, Metropolit. *Slova i rechi. [Sermons and Speeches]*. 4 vols. Moscow: The Moscow Patriarchate, 1947, 1949, 1954, 1957.

Nikol'ski, Konstantin. *Posobie k izucheniiu ustava bohosluzheniia pravoslavnoi tzerkvi. [Aid for Learning the Rubics of Divine Services of the Orthodox Church]* 6th ed. revised. St. Petersburg: Gosudaratvenaia Tipografiia, 1900.

Ostrogorsky, George. *History of the Byzantine State*. Translated by Joan Hussey. Oxford: A. R. Mowbray and Co., Ltd., 1956.

Panfilov, T., and Skibitski, M. (eds.). *Sputnik ateista. [Sputnik of the Atheist]* Moscow: Gosudarstvennoe Izdatel'stvo Politicheskoi Literaturi, 1961.

Pares, Bernard. *The Fall of the Russian Monarchy*. New York: Vintage Books, 1961.

————. *Russia: Between Reform and Revolution*. New York: Schocken Books, 1962.

Parsons, Talcott; Shils, Edward; Naegele, Kaspar D.; Pitts, Jesse R. (eds.). *Theories of Society: Foundations of Modern Sociological Theory*. 2 vols. New York: The Free Press of Glencoe, Inc., 1961.

Patriarchal, l'Exarchat Russe. *Chudesa i pritchti Hristovi*. [*Miracles and Parables of Christ*] Paris: l'Exarchat patriarchal russe en Europe occidentale, 1962.

Patriarchate, The Moscow. *The Russian Orthodox Church: Organization, Situation, and Activity*. Moscow: The Moscow Patriarchate, no date given.

———. *The Russian Orthodox Church in the Fight for Peace: Decisions, Epistles, Appeals and Articles 1948–1950*. Moscow: The Moscow Patriarchate, 1950.

Patriarchiia, Moskovskaia. *Dejaniia soveshaniia glav i predstavitelei avtokefal'nikh pravoslavnikh tzerkvei v sviazi s prazdnovaniem 500 letiia avtokefalii russkoi pravoslavnoi tzerkvi 8–18 iuliia 1948 goda* [*The Acts and Conferences of Heads and Representatives of the Autocephalous Orthodox Churches in Conjunction with the 500th Anniversary of the Autocephaly of the Russian Orthodox Church 8–18 July 1948*]. 2 vols. Moscow: The Moscow Patriarchate, 1949.

———. *Patriarch Sergei i eho dukhovnoe nasledstvo*. [*Patriarch Sergei and His Spiritual Legacy*]. Moscow: The Moscow Patriarchate, 1947.

———. *Pravda o Religii v Rossii*. [*The Truth About Religion in Russia*]. Moscow: The Moscow Patriarchate, 1942.

———. *Russkaia pravoslavnaia tzerkov: ustroistvo, polozhenie, deiatel'nost*. [*The Russian Orthodox Church: Organization, Situation and Activity*]. Moscow: The Moscow Patriarchate, 1958.

———. *Sluzhebnik*. [*Book of Offices*]. Moscow: The Moscow Patriarchate, 1958.

———. *Tipicon*. [*Book of Rules*]. Moscow: Synodal'naia Tipografiia, 1906.

———. *Trebnik*. [*Book of Needs*]. Moscow: The Moscow Patriarchate, 1956.

Pfeffer, Leo. *Church, State and Freedom*. Boston: The Beacon Press, 1953.

Prokofiev, V. I. *Ateism russkikh revolutzionikh demokratov*. [*The Atheism of the Russian Revolutionary Democrats*]. Moscow: Gospolitizdat, 1952.

Rauch, Georg von. *History of Soviet Russia*. Translated by Peter Jacobson and Annette Jacobson. New York: Frederick A. Praeger, 1960.

Reyburn, Hugh Y. *The Story of the Russian Church*. London: Andrew Melrose Ltd., 1924.

Riley, Athelstan (ed.). *Birbeck and the Russian Church*. New York: The Macmillan Company, 1917.

Runciman, Steven. *Byzantine Civilization*. New York: Meridian House, 1956.

———. *The Eastern Schism*. Oxford: The Clarendon Press, 1956.

Schaff, Philip, and Wace, Henry (ed.). *The Nicene and Post Nicene Fathers*. Vol. IX. Grand Rapids: William Eerdmans Pulishing Company, 1955.

Schapiro, Leonard. *The Communist Party of the Soviet Union*. New York: Random House, 1960.

Schwars, Fred. *You Can Trust the Communists (to be Communists)*. Englewood Cliffs: Prentice-Hall, Inc., 1962.

Schwartz, Harry (ed.). *The Many Faces of Communism*. New York: Berkeley Medallion Books, 1962.

Schwartzchild, Leopold. *Karl Marx: The Red Prussian*. New York: Grosset and Dunlap, 1947.

Seligman, Edwin R. A., and Johnson, Alvin (eds.). *Selections from the Encyclopaedia of Social Sciences*. New York: The Macmillan Company, 1938.

Selznick, Philip. *The Organizational Weapon: A Study of Bolshevik Strategy and Tactics*. Glencoe, Ill.: Free Press, 1960.

Sheen, Fulton J. *Communism and the Conscience of the West*. New York: The Bobbs-Merrill Company, 1948.

Shub, Boris, and Quint, Bernard. *Since Stalin: A Photo History of Our Time*. New York: Swan Publications Co., Inc., 1951.

Shub, David. *Lenin*. New York: Mentor Books, 1960.

Shuster, George N. *Religion Behind the Iron Curtain*. New York: The Macmillan Company, 1954.

Sokolof, D. *A Manual of the Orthodox Church's Divine Services*. Jordanville, N.Y.: Printing Shop of St. Iov of Pochaev, 1962.

Solberg, Richard W. *God and Caesar in East Germany.* New York: The Macmillan Company, 1961.
Solovyev, Vladimir. *Russia and the Universal Church.* London: The Centenary Press, 1948.
Spinka, Matthew. *Christianity Confronts Communism.* London: Ebenezer Baylie and Son, Ltd., 1938.
———. *The Church in Soviet Russia.* New York: Oxford University Press, 1956.
Stanley, Arthur Penrhyn. *Lectures on the History of the Eastern Church.* New York: Scribner, Armstrong and Company, 1873.
Stepanov, Skvortzov, I. I. *Blagochestivie razmishleniia* [*Devout Reflections*]. Moscow: Gospolitizdat, 1959.
Sumarev, P. I. (ed.). *Russkie pisateli o religii.* [*Russian Writers About Religion*]. Moscow: Sovetskaia Rossiia, 1959.
Synod, Most Holy. *Octoechos.* [*Book of Eight Tones*]. London: J. Dauy and Sons, 1898.
Szczesniak, Boleslaw (ed.). *The Russian Revolution and Religion: A Collection of Documents Concerning the Suppression of Religion by the Communists 1917–1925.* Notre Dame: Notre Dame University Press, 1959.
Timasheff, Nicholas S. *Religion in Soviet Russia.* London: The Religious Book Club, 1943.
———. *Sociological Theory: Its Nature and Growth.* New York: Random House, 1957.
Treadgold, Donald W. *Twentieth Century Russia.* Chicago: Rand McNally, 1959.
Triska, Jan F. (ed.). *Soviet Communism: Programs and Rules.* Chandler Publishing Company, 1962.
Turner, Ralph M., and Killian, Lewis M. *Collective Behavior.* Englewood Cliffs, N.J.: Prentice-Hall, Inc., 1957.
Ulich, Robert. *The Education of Nations.* Cambridge: Harvard University Press, 1961.
Utechin, S. V. *Concise Encyclopedia of Russia.* London: J. N. Dent and Sons, Ltd., 1961.
Valentinov, A. A. *Chornaia kniga: shturm nebes.* [*The Black Book: Storming of the Heavens*]. London: Privately printed, 1925.
Vassiliev, A. A. *History of the Byzantine Empire.* 2 vols., Madison: The University of Wisconsin Press, 1958.
Veniamin, Archiepiskop. *Novaia Skrizhal'.* [New Tablets]. St. Petersburg: Edward Weimar Tipografiia, 1857.
Vil'chinski, V. P. (ed.). *Russkoe narodnoe poeticheskoe tvorchestvo protiv tzerkvi i religii.* [*Russian People's Poetical Creative Works against the Church and Religion*]. Moscow: Academy of Sciences, U.S.S.R., 1961.
Vladislavlev, Protoierei. *Obiasnenie Bogosluzheniia sviatoi pravoslavnoi tzerkvi.* [Explanation of the Divine Services of the Holy Orthodox Church]. St. Petersburg: I. L. Tuzov, 1905.
Waddams, M. H. *Anglo-Russian Theological Conference: Moscow, July 1956.* London: The Faith Press, 1957.
Walissewski, K. *Paul the First of Russia: The Son of Catherine the Great.* Philadelphia: J. B. Lippincott Company, 1913.
———. *Peter the Great.* Translated by Lady Mary Loyd. London: William Heinemann, 1898.
Watson, Hugh, Seaton. *The Decline of Imperial Russia: 1885–1914.* 5th ed. New York: Frederick A. Praeger, 1961.
———. *The Pattern of Communist Revolution: A History of World Communism.* London: Methuen and Co., Ltd., 1953.
Weber, Max. *Basic Concepts in Sociology.* Translated by H. P. Secher. New York: The Citadel Press, 1962.
Weidlé, Wladimir. *Russia: Absent and Present.* Translated by A. Gordon Smith. New York: Vintage Books, 1961.
Whyte, William Foote, *Men at Work.* Homewood, Ill.: The Dorsey Press, Inc., and Richard D. Irwin, Inc., 1961.

Wolfe, Bertram D. *Three Who Made a Revolution.* Boston: Beacon Press, 1960.
Yesipov, B. P., and Goncharov, N. K. *I Want to Be Like Stalin.* Translated by George S. Counts and Nucia P. Lodge. New York: The John Day Company, 1947.
Zaitsev, Kiril. *Pravoslavnaia tzerkov v sovetskoi rossi.* [*The Orthodox Church in Soviet Russia*]. Shanghai: Privately printed, 1947.
Zavedsev, Petr. *Polnee rukovodetvo dlia podgotovki k ekzamenu na sviashennika.* [*Complete Guidance for Preparing for the Examination of a Priest*]. 2d ed. Moscow: Bol'shaia Presnia, 1912.
Zernov, Nicholas. *Eastern Christendom.* New York: G. P. Putnams Sons, 1961.
———. *Orthodox Encounter.* London: James Clark and Co., Ltd., 1961.
———. *The Russians and Their Church.* New York: The Macmillan Co., 1945.
Zetlir, Mikhail. *The Decembrists.* Translated by George Panin. New York: International Universities Press, Inc., 1958.
Zvegintzov, C. *Our Mother Church: Her Offices and Worship.* Compiled from Standard Russian Textbooks. London: S.P.C.K., 1948.

Public Documents

U. S. Department of Health, Welfare and Education. *Soviet Education Programs: Foundations, Curriculums, Teacher Preparation.* Washington: U. S. Government Printing Office, 1960.
U. S. Department of State Publication. *Soviet World Outlook.* Publication No. 6836 (European and British Commonwealth Series 56), Washington: July, 1959.
U. S. House of Representatives, Committee on Un-American Activities. *The Communist Conspiracy: Strategy and Tactics of World Communism.* Report No. 2240, 84th Cong., 2d Sess., May 29, 1956.
———. *The Communist Conspiracy: Strategy and Tactics of World Communism.* Report No. 2241, 84th Cong., 2d Sess., May 29, 1956.
———. *The Communist Conspiracy: Strategy and Tactics of World Communism.* Report No. 2242, 84th Cong., 2d Sess., May 29, 1956.
———. *Communist Persecution of Churches in Red China and Northern Korea.* 86th Cong., 1st Sess., 1959.
———. *Communist Psychological Warfare (Brainwashing).* 85th Cong., 2d Sess., 1958.
———. *The Crimes of Khrushchev.* Part 2, 86th Cong., 1st Sess., 1959.
———. *The Crimes of Khrushchev.* Part 3, 86th Cong., 1st Sess., 1959.
———. *The Crimes of Khrushchev.* Part 4, 86th Cong., 1st Sess., 1959.
———. *The Crimes of Khrushchev.* Part 5, 86th Cong., 1st Sess., 1959.
———. *The Crimes of Khrushchev.* Part 6, 86th Cong., 1st Sess., 1959.
———. *The Crimes of Khrushchev.* Part 7, 86th Cong., 2d Sess., 1960.
———. *Facts on Communism: The Communist Ideology.* Report No. 336, 86th Cong., 2d Sess., December, 1959, Vol. I.
———. *Facts on Communism: The Soviet Union, From Lenin to Khrushchev.* Report No. 336. 86th Cong., 2d Sess., December 1959, Vol. II.
———. *The Ideological Fallacies of Communism.* 85th Cong., 1st Sess., 1958.
———. *International Communism (The Communist Mind).* 85th Cong., 1st Sess., 1957.
———. *World Communist Movement: Selective Chronology 1918–1945.* 79th Cong., 2d Sess., 1946, Vol. I.
———. *Hearings Before the Committee on Un-American Activities on the Kremlin's Espionage and Terror Organizations.* 86th Cong., 1st Sess., 1959.
U. S. Senate, Committee on the Judiciary. *The Church and State Under Communism.* Part I, The U.S.S.R., 89th Cong., 1st Sess., 1964, Vol. I.
———. *The Church and State Under Communism.* Part II and Part III, The U.S.S.R., 89th Cong., 1st Sess., 1965, Vol. I.

————. *The Church and State under Communism.* Rumania, Bulgaria, Albania. 89th Cong., 1st Sess., 1965, Vol. II.
————. *The Church and State under Communism.* Yugoslavia. 89th Cong., 1st Sess., 1965, Vol. III.
————. *The Church and State Under Communism.* Lithuania, Latvia, and Estonia. 89th Cong., 1st Sess., 1965, Vol. IV.
————. *Communist Controls on Religious Activity.* 86th Cong., 1st Sess., 1959.
————. *Contradictions of Communism.* 86th Cong., 1st Sess., 1959.
————. *Expose of Soviet Espionage May 1960.* Document No. 114, 86th Cong., 2d Sess., 1960.
————. *Khrushchev's Strategy and Its Meaning for America.* 86th Cong., 2d Sess., 1960.
————. *The Technique of Soviet Propaganda.* 86th Cong., 2d Sess., 1960.
————. *Wordsmanship: Semantics as a Communist Weapon.* 87th Cong., 2d Sess., 1961.
U. S. Senate, Senator Hubert H. Humphrey. *Khrushchev on the Shifting Balance of World Forces.* Document No. 57, 86th Cong., 1st Sess., 1959.

Annuals, Articles and Periodicals

Current Digest of the Soviet Press: Consisting of translations from Soviet periodicals with bibliographical index of Soviet newspapers. New York: Joint Committee on Slavic Studies, 1949–1963.
Ezhegodnik muzei istorii religii i ateisma (The Annual of the Museum of History of Religion and Atheism). Vol. II, Moscow: Academy of Sciences, U.S.S.R., 1958.
————. Vol. III, 1959.
————. Vol. IV, 1960.
Gazeti i zhurnali SSSR na 1963 god. (Newspapers and Journals, U.S.S.R., for 1963). Moscow: Mezhdunarodnaia Kniga, 1963.
Pravoslavnj Tzerkovnj Kalendar. (The Orthodox Church Calendar). Moscow: The Moscow Patriarchate, 1945–1962.
Institute for the Study of the U.S.S.R. *Religion in the U.S.S.R.* Edited by Boris Ivanov. Translated and edited by James Larkin. (Series I, No. 59, July, 1960.) Munich: Carl Gerber Grafische Betriebe K. G., 1960.
Syracuse Herald Journal. June 28, 1963.
Zhurnal Moskovskoi Patriarchii. (Journal of the Moscow Patriarchate). Moscow: The Moscow Patriarchate, 1943–1963.

Reports

Anderson, Wroe, *et al. Meeting the Russians: American Quakers Visit the Soviet Union.* A Report Prepared by the Delegation. Philadelphia: American Friends Service Committee, 1956.
Andreev, Ivan. *O polozhenii pravoslavnoi tzerkvi v sovetskom souze. (Regarding the Conditions of the Orthodox Church in the Soviet Union).* A Report to the Bishop Sobor, Jordanville, New York, December 7, 1950. Prepared by the Holy Trinity Monastery, Jordanville, N.Y. 1951.
Antonia, Episcop. *O polozhenii tzerkvi v sovetskoi Rossii i duhovnoi zhizni russkaho naroda. (Regarding the Conditions of the Church in Soviet Russia and the Spiritual Life of the People).* A Report to the Bishop Sobor, Jordanville, New York, 1959. Prepared by the Holy Trinity Monastery, Jordanville, N.Y., 1960.
Pomazansky, Michael. *The Church of Christ and the Contemporary Movement for Unification in Christianity.* A Report to the XV Diocese Assembly. Prepared by the Holy Trinity Monastery, Jordanville, New York, 1962.

Communist Periodicals of the U.S.S.R.

Bol'shevik, (Bolshevik), 1948–1951.
Izvestia, (The News), 1950–1962.
Komsomol'skaia pravda, (Komsomolskaia Truth), 1950–1959.
Kultura i zhisn, (Culture and Life), 1951–1962.
Kulturno prosvititel'naia rabota, (Culturally Enlightening Work), 1949–1953.
Literaturnaiia gazeta, (Literary News), 1949–1960.
Nauka i zhisn, (Science and Life), 1951–1962.
Pravda, (The Truth), 1950–1962.
Sovetskaia kultura, (Soviet Culture), 1955–1959.
Sovetskaia litva, (Soviet Latvia), 1955–1956.
Sovetskaia pedagogika, (Soviet Pedagogy), 1949–1952.
Sovetsky flot, (Soviet Fleet), 1955–1957.
Trud, (Labor), 1954–1958.
Vestnik akademii nauk, (Messenger of the Academy of Sciences), 1954–1957.
Vestnik vysshei shkoli, (Messenger of the Higher Schools), 1955–1958.
Voprosy filosofii, (Questions of Philosophy), 1961–1962.

Index

Academies, *see* Education, Theological
Academy of Sciences (U.S.S.R.), 90,
96
"Administration of the Church, Situation of the," *see* Regulations of 1945
Adrian, Patriarch, 1, 2
Alexei, Patriarch, 39, 44, 73, 82, 106;
patriotic activities, 34, 54–59, 63
Alivizantos, Professor, 66
All-Russian Extraordinary Commission
for Combating Counter-Revolution,
15
Anathematizing Proclamation (Tikhon), 10
Andrei, Archbishop of Saratov, 32;
statement of 1941, 144–45
Anti-religious activities, 23, 25–27, 85,
103–104
Anti-religious education, 27
Anti-religious publications, 83, 85–86,
91–97, 112
Antonin, Bishop of Living Church, 19,
20
Armour, Norman, 16
Ateism, obshchestvo i religia (book), 93
Atheism, 14, 15, 87, 89–91, 99, 100
Athenagoras, Patriarch, 63–64

Biblia dlya veruushih i neveruushih
(book), 92
Blagochestivie ramishleniia (paperback
book), 96

Calendar, Orthodox Church, 82
Calendar reform, 9 (note 1)
Children: religious education, 104, 119
Church Affairs, Department of, 35
Church and State, Separation of: Fifth
Party Congress, 12; Laws of 1917, 8;
Laws of 1918, 117–118; Laws of
1922, 119–120. *See also* Funds for
religious organizations

Church and State relations: Czarist
period, 1–4; Karpov, 35, 41, 45–46;
regulations of 1945, 36, 46; restrictions on the Church, 10, 80–81, 98,
108
Church statistics, 3, 4, 9, 42, 43–44, 80
Clergy, 27, 34, 42, 80, 94–95, 107;
education 69–80, 112
Communism: philosophy of religion, 23,
83–84, 98–105
Communist Manifesto (Marx), 99
Communist Youth Movement, 25
"Concerning Religious Associations," 26
Constantinople, Patriarch of, 1, 2
Council of Ministers, 36
Criminal Code Regarding Religion
(1922), 119–120
Cults, Ministry of (U.S.S.R.), 36, 49,
91

Dejaniia soveschaniia glav i predstavitelei avtokefal'nikh pravoslavnikh tzerkvei (book), 83
Diocesan Hierarch: regulations, 138,
141
Divorce, 8
Dobrolubov, Nicolas A., 96
Dorotheus, Metropolitan of Athens, 58

Ecumenical activities, 59–63, 65–68
Education, Theological, 69–80, 112, 119
Efrem II, Catholicos Patriarch of
Georgia, 62
Excommunication, 11
Ezhegodnik muzea istorii religii i ateisma (annual), 92

Famine, 18
Filofei of Pskov, 44
"Forty-Eight Paragraphs," *see* Regulations of 1945
Fotii, Archbishop, 56

159